Out Of The Box Retirement

Creative Ideas, Role Models, And Possibilities

To Joe:
Here's to an
inspiring retiring
Jeanne
Walsh

Retirement Coaches Association

Table of Contents

Introduction

As you might expect, I can't write a traditional introduction for an out-of-the-box-type retirement planning book. It just wouldn't work, so let me jump right in by asking you a game-changing question:

"Whose retirement rules are you following and why are you following them?"

It's an important question for several reasons. First, you have probably never been asked it before. That means you have to immediately start thinking differently about the topic.

Second, people often follow a herd mentality. They go with the flow and do what everyone else is doing. In other words, they are following someone else's directions toward retirement and may not even realize it.

By blindly following others, many people end up getting to retirement but can feel lost or out of place. They were handed a set of directions that suggested they need to save a specific amount of money and work until a certain age, and then by leaving work they would be happy and fulfilled in retirement.

But that's not how it works, and is a major problem with traditional retirement planning. It assumes if you get the dollars and cents right, that everything else will fall into place.

Think of it like following your GPS exactly as it guides you and then once it says, "You have arrived," you look around and you're not where you thought you were going to be.

This is exactly why we created the Retirement Coaches Association and are writing this book. As a group of highly trained and specialized professionals we recognize the need to change retirement planning.

We know from experience and working with individuals, couples, groups, and organizations that people need a written plan for the non-financial aspects of retirement including things like replacing their work identity, filling their time, and staying relevant and connected as well as mentally and physically active.

In other words, we need to insert some creative ideas and energies into the process. This is exactly why we brought together some of the top retirement coaches from our industry for this unique project.

We want to not only encourage you to set aside the old directions you have been following up to this point, but to also provide you with fresh ideas, positive role models, and new possibilities. An approach that is designed to help you better prepare and balance out the financial parts with the more personal aspects.

On the following pages, you will find our life's work including chapters on people, places, and things that have shaped us and the clients we work with. Don't feel confined to following the normal page rules or reading this book in sequential order. Stroll through the material at your own pace, taking time to stop and enjoy this new and up-to-date perspective on life in retirement.

We are here to make an impact and help you thrive in your transition from work life to home life. Please don't hesitate to share your thoughts and feedback with us at www.RetirementCoachesAssociation.org, or feel free to connect with individual authors based on their contact information available at the end of each chapter.

Sincerely,

Robert Laura

Founder, Retirement Coaches Association

M And A: Mindset + Action
By Michele Fantt Harris

In business, when you hear the term "M and A" you automatically think of mergers and acquisitions. M and A's are tools businesses use to achieve a greater share of the market and to enhance the nature of their business or competitive position. A merger is a consolidation of two entities into one company, while an acquisition is where one entity takes ownership or control of another entity's assets.

To have a successful merger and acquisition, the combined company must develop a comprehensive strategy to navigate the troublesome waters of combining two companies into one.

For a successful retirement, one must have an M and A as well. The retiree must carefully plan their retirement prior to taking the leap of faith into the unknown. A successful retirement requires a change in one's mindset and action on the part of the retiree.

A successful retiree is one who has changed their awareness and is curious and ready to explore new territory. Once the retiree has shifted their awareness, it is then time to act. Action must be paired with awareness. To be fully aware and take no action will leave the retiree in the same place – the starting point.

The keystone of a successful retirement is personal and/or professional growth that contributes to one's personal happiness and satisfaction. One's mindset includes the mental and emotional structures that shape the person's perceptions, interpretations and actions.

The mindset encompasses how you think, make decisions, behave, and what you like and dislike in yourself and others. One's personal preferences can be influenced by how you and others feel about you and your abilities.

Before two organizations plan a merger, they first assess the infrastructure before developing a strategic plan to advance the joining of the two organizations. In a successful retirement, the retiree needs to assess their values, interests, skills, and abilities. First, potential retirees need to assess their current state of mind by asking themselves the following questions:

- What are my interests? What do I really enjoy doing?
- What type of environment and activities attract me at this stage of my life? Does it require me to relocate?
- What are my personal values? What is important to me at this stage of my life?
- Do I want or need to continue paid employment? What do I want my life to look like 5 or 10 years from now?

- Are my personal preferences in line with my lifestyle needs (including location, work or pleasure needs, and financial income)?
- What drives and motivates me to action? Does my high or low motivation require me to make sacrifices in other areas of my life?
- Do I believe that I can accomplish my future goals? If not, what is hindering me from achieving my dreams?
- Am I moving in my desired direction? If not, why?
- Are my future goals in alignment with the goals of my spouse or partner?
- Have I taken stock of my life now in relation to my past, present, and future goals, as well as dreams and needs?
- If you want to continue working, are you considering entrepreneurship? How well do your skills and interests support that new direction and change?
- Are you living your passion? Do you wake up ready to achieve your personal and professional fulfillment? Are you limiting yourself from achieving your passion because of money, skills, and what others say?
- What is the legacy that I want to leave to my children, community, and world?

An important part of any career or life transition is to assess one's values. Values are the beliefs that we hold most dear. Values determine what is important and meaningful to you and provide a roadmap to one's lifetime decisions and choices.

These values guide potential retirees in their future plans. Research shows the more aligned your values are with your work or retirement endeavors, the more satisfied and fulfilling your retirement will be. By identifying one's core values, a potential retiree is better prepared to identify personal and professional development opportunities for retirement. They are able to ask:

- How does my future retirement endeavor align with my core values?
- Are there volunteer opportunities or paid assignments that align well with my core values?
- How do I prepare myself for a future role that aligns with my personal values?

See the final section of this chapter for a list of values that you may find helpful in doing this type of exploration.[1]

Once we take the time to review our strengths, values and passions, we are developing the infrastructure of our mindset. The key is to build a mindset of prosperity and not famine. Steven Covey in *The 7 Habits of Highly Effective People*, refers to "scarcity mentality" and "abundance mentality." A famished mindset or scarcity mindset feels that there will never be enough money, resources, recognition, etc.

Conversely, the prosperity mindset or abundance mentality flows out of a deep inner sense of personal worth and well-being. A prosperous mindset feels that there are plenty of resources for everyone, and the prosperous mindset is open to possibilities, options, alternatives, and creativity. When people cultivate a prosperous mindset, they say "yes" to opportunities for growth even if they don't have the skills for the task or they feel unprepared.

Retirees with positive mindsets will see new opportunities as a way to pause, reflect, learn, do and grow. With a positive mindset, you will become more aware and will take greater responsibility for action, growth, and development. When you focus on your strengths and what is important to you, you will see a visible change in your mindset. There will be a new hope and confidence in your mindset and attitude. You will act with meaning and purpose.[2]

Remind yourself of your values every day. Tape a list of your values to your bathroom mirror. Create a screensaver on your laptop or a wallpaper for your smartphone with a picture that represents one of your values. Choose a song that represents one or more of your values and listen to it at least twice per day.

Now that you have the M, it is time to move to the A – action. Take your values, passions and strengths and apply them to everyday life. Let your values be your guiding principles, for they will give you energy and enthusiasm.

The first action step is to be mindful of your values and to examine if you are living by your values and with meaning in every aspect of your life. Examine every aspect of your life, including marriage/partner/significant other, family and relationships, career/work, finances, health, recreation and hobbies, spiritual life, and your physical environment.

As you approach retirement, you need to rate your level of satisfaction with each area of your life. Rate each area in a range from 1 to 10 with 10 meaning you are highly satisfied and 1 meaning you are not satisfied. Don't take too long to rate each area of your life; use your gut response. Listening to your intuition gives you a deeper look into your values. Your gut reaction will tell you to act, but your values will tell you why to act.

Look at the areas of your life where you score 7 or less. You cannot change everything in a day, so select one or two areas to work on at a time. Start with one area where there is "low hanging fruit." By tackling an easy area of change, you will give yourself immediate success and confidence to handle the more challenging areas of your life that need to change.

Assess where you are in each area of your life and clarify where you want to be. Develop a vision of where you want to be. Create a goal and action steps to help you achieve your goal.

Identify any limiting beliefs or saboteurs that may get in the way of you achieving your goal. Shirzad Chamine, author of the book *Positive Intelligence: Why Only 20% of Teams and Individuals Achieve*

Their True Potential, and How You Can Achieve Yours, created a free online assessment that helps individuals identify their unique "saboteurs," as well as understand the master saboteur, which he calls "The Judge."

The Judge is the universal Saboteur that afflicts everyone. It is the one that beats you up repeatedly over mistakes or shortcomings, warns you obsessively about future risks, wakes you up in the middle of the night worrying, and gets you fixated on what is wrong with your life or others. The Judge is our greatest internal enemy.

Take the free assessment at https://www.positiveintelligence.com/assessments to learn your saboteurs and how to proactively use them to help you to live your dreams with compassion.[3]

Now, rework your goal as a SMART goal – one that is specific (states exactly what is to be achieved), measurable (establishes clear definitions to help you measure if the goal is reached), action-oriented (described using action words and an outline of the steps needed to accomplish the goal), realistic (reasonable and attainable), and time bound (with a definition for the amount of time needed to start and finish the goal).

Write each of your goals and post them where you will see them daily. Always state your goals positively. State changes for yourself and not for others. The goal should be large enough to stretch you but within the realm of possibility to achieve it.[4]

Now that you have created your goal, you need to visualize it. Create a mental picture of what you want to achieve. If you are more attracted to images, cut out pictures and create a vision board. For example, if you have decided that you want to relocate to a warmer climate when you retire, visualize or create a vision board of exactly the place where you will retire.

In what state will you live? Will you live by the water, in the city, or in a rural location? Will you live in an apartment, townhouse, single family home, or farm? Will you own, buy, or lease your new home? What will the community look like – a senior retirement community, diverse community with people of various backgrounds and ages, pet-friendly area, or gated community? How will you travel to the community – public transportation, by car, or walking? What amenities are in your community – banks, restaurants, post office, movie theaters, gardens, parks, or grocery stores? Visualize yourself in the community or add your photograph to the vision board.

Give life to your goal. Visualize and verbally affirm your goal every day. Believe in your vision. What we believe in, we will create. The more you visualize your goal you will attract circumstances and people to help bring your goal to fruition. As you continue to visualize the relocation goal, you will begin to notice more advertisements for communities like the one you visualize for your future. You will attract persons who live in similar communities or real estate agents who sell or rent properties in communities that you like.

Create affirmations or statements declaring what changes you want to see in your life. Write your affirmations in positive statements. Make them specific and to the point. State the affirmations as if they already exist and make them personal with your name, "I," or "me."

Make your affirmations exciting and enticing as well as in the realm of being achievable. For example, an affirmation of the relocation goal might say, "I am living in a gated, 55-and-older community, in a two-story townhouse overlooking the peaceful Pacific Ocean in beautiful San Diego, California." See and read your affirmations daily as you visualize your future change.

The constant attention to your goal will take it from visualization to manifestation or action and your goal will become your main day-to-day focus. Affirm, visualize and energize your goals daily!

If you find yourself not moving ahead fast enough, getting bogged down, or wanting to accomplish more goals, consider hiring a retirement coach. One of the best ways to move ahead with your goals is to designate time with a retirement coach who will hold you accountable for the goals that you set.

Two great resources for retirement coaches are the Retirement Coaches Association (www.retirementcoachesassociation.org) or Retirement Options, Inc. (www.retirementoptions.com).

If you are seeking to make a career change during retirement, contact The Academies, Inc., (www.theacademies.com/find-a-coach) to find a list of certified career management coaches. Explore the directory for these three organizations. Review the bios of the coaches, contact them and conduct a mini interview to help you find a compatible coach. To understand coaching, ask the potential coach for a "trial session." This free session will help you understand the coaching process and your involvement and responsibilities.

Coaches can help you achieve and maximize your goals to reach your highest potential in every aspect of your life! You are at the beginning of your retirement journey. All you need to do is to take the first step!

What Are My Values?

Values are the beliefs that ground you and are very special to you personally. Your values determine what is important and meaningful to you; they guide your decisions in your career, relationships, and life. Rate each value from 1-5, from least to most important. Identify your top five values, with 5 being the most important core value, and 1 being the least important.

_____ **Building a Better World:** Do something which contributes to improving the world we live in.

_____ **Helping Others:** Become directly involved in helping other people, either individually or in small groups.

_____ **Win by Competing:** Engage in activities which pit my abilities against others.

_____ **Influencing People:** Influence the attitudes or opinions of other people.

_____ **Learning New Things:** Have freedom to engage in the pursuit of knowledge and understanding.

_____ **Becoming the Best in My Field:** Achieve mastery in whatever work you do.

_____ **Being Able to Express Myself Creatively:** Engage in creative artistic expression.

_____ **Having a Beautiful Environment:** Create or surround yourself with a beauty that you can appreciate and enjoy.

_____ **Having Lots of Variety:** Engage in work activities which frequently change.

_____ **Receiving Recognition:** Receive recognition for the high quality of your work.

_____ **Having Excitement and Adventure:** Experience a high degree of (or frequent) excitement in the course of your work and have work duties which require frequent risk-taking.

_____ **Making Lots of Money:** Achieve very great monetary rewards for your work.

_____ **Being Physically Active:** Use your physical capabilities in your work.

_____ **Having Autonomy and Freedom:** Determine the nature of your work without significant direction from others.

_____ **Moral Integrity:** Engage in work that maintains a set of moral standards which you feel are very important.

_____ **Have a Community at Work:** Be a part of a team that helps each other and sometimes shares activities outside of work.

_____ **Work/Life Balance:** Meet your work responsibilities in a timeframe that matches with other priority activities in your life.

_____ **Having Stability and Job Security:** Establish work routine and job duties that are largely predictable. Feel assured of keeping your job and receiving satisfactory compensation.

_____ **Other**

About The Author

Michele Fantt Harris, SHRM-SCP, SPHR, ACC, is EVP, HR, for the National Cooperative Bank in

Washington, D.C. A seasoned HR professional, this is her seventh anthology. Her latest, *Imagination@Work* (Silver Tree Publishing, 2018), is available on Amazon. A certified retirement coach and a certified career management coach through The Academies, Inc., she serves on the Leadership Center for Excellence Board of Regents. She received her BA from the University of Maryland, Baltimore County, an MAS from Johns Hopkins, and a JD from the University of Baltimore. A certified senior HR expert, she teaches at Prince Georges Community College and Catholic University. Contact her at Michele.Harris19@gmail.com.

Notes

[1] *Talent Match: Navigating Your Career*, www.itsinc.net. This exercise is used with permission of its developer, Lynn Ware of Integral Talent Systems. A version of this exercise appears in the participant guide and learning journal for the ITS program.

[2] Stephen R. Covey, *The 7 Habits of Highly Effective People: Restoring the Character Ethic* (New York: Free Press, 2004).

[3] Shirzad Chamine, *Positive Intelligence: Why Only 20% of Teams and Individuals Achieve Their True Potential and How You Can Achieve Yours* (California: Greenleaf Book Press, 2012).

[4] Michele Fantt Harris, et al., "Coaching In the Workplace," *Imagination@Work*, (Kenosha, WI: Silver Tree Publishing, 2019), 31-43.

Jaw Dropping Ideas For Retirement
By Robert Laura

I was trained as a traditional financial advisor over two decades ago, and let's just say that the terms "creative" or "out of the box" were not too popular back then. In fact, retirement wasn't even considered a journey or treated as this ideal phase of life. It was essentially a finish line that we were supposed to help our clients reach by following specific steps and rules.

It was a pretty cut-and-dry approach, or so I thought. Five years into my logical, left-brained advisory approach, I met a couple who were thinking about retirement. She was a flight attendant for a major airline, and he worked on an assembly line for a Big Three auto maker.

Initially, the meeting went as planned. They shared all the information about their savings, Social Security, and pensions. We also talked about their plans for life after work and their big goal was to travel 6-8 times a year, especially during harsh Michigan winters.

Now, many people have travel as a goal for their retirement years, but most of the time they plan to take one or two big trips a year and sprinkle in a weekend getaway or two. So, this couple was definitely shooting for the stars and would need some hefty savings to accomplish it.

As it turns out, my worst fears were confirmed after I ran their numbers. There was no way this couple could retire and hit their travel goals. It just wasn't possible, and I was the lucky guy who got to crush their dreams and tell them that they could retire but essentially couldn't leave the house.

This was the first time I had to deliver bad news, so I tried to come up with some creative ways to do it. The best I could do was, "Yes, you can retire but your travel options may be restricted." The reports I had generated suggested that they could spend about $3,000 a year on travel, not the $15,000 or more I projected that they would need.

When I delivered the news, I was expecting a sad or angry face, and maybe even a little push back on the calculations I used. But that didn't happen. They were strangely happy, in fact the wife said, "That's just about where we thought we would need to be."

I was confused. I had no idea how they were going to travel 6-8 times a year on a $3,000 budget. My eyes were opened when the couple explained their crafty plan.

"We don't need a $15,000 travel budget. Since I retired from the airline, our plane tickets are $25 per person as long as we fly standby … and once we officially retire, a friend of mine is going to get me a job working the front desk at a local hotel chain a couple days a week and John will be working part-time as a porter for a rental car agency." She added, "It will keep us busy during the week and then we can pretty much travel, stay in different places, and get around town for next to nothing."

I was in shock. I'm sure I was sitting there with my mouth wide open. After working with literally hundreds of people up to that point, I had never met anyone with a plan that went outside of the traditional dollars and cents. Someone who was planning on using their skills and time as currency instead of relying on personal savings and investments. It was enlightening and opened up a whole new world of possibilities that I had never considered before.

That's definitely one of the benefits of being a financial professional. You get to work with and see first-hand how people not only plan to get to retirement, but also see what they actually do during it. Several years after my first creative experience, I had the good fortune to meet another couple that was ahead of their time. They had been retired for almost 10 years and were looking for a new financial advisor since their previous one had just retired.

Our conversation was going well and, being curious about both their previous work life and time in retirement, I asked, "How did you know it was time to retire?"

The couple looked at each other, chuckled, and Jerry spoke up, "We knew it was time to retire when we were out with a group of friends who were also nearing retirement and we all decide to play a retirement game."

Now he had my full attention because I had no idea there was any kind of retirement game.

He continued on, "We went around the table and each person shared something they were going to do once they retired. We won the game that night because we had played with some friends before and so we spent some time thinking about and writing down all the things we wanted to do once we retired."

Once again, I'm sure my mouth was wide open. I was thinking, "What do you mean you thought about and wrote down all the things you want to do once you retired?" Like many people, I assumed retirement just magically happened – that people just figured it out as they went along and that it didn't require any real planning, time, or effort.

The couple continued, "We have learned that if you don't have at least 12-15 major things you each want to do once you retire, then you're probably not ready."

I was floored because it was the first time I had anyone suggest that a decision to retire included aspects that went beyond the investment charts and graphs. I hate to admit it, but up to that point, I had no idea that there was this mental or more personal side of retirement.

To top things off, as the couple was leaving, he handed me a business card. I was caught off guard once again because he had been retired for 10 years and I had no idea why a retired person would be handing out an old business card.

So, I was quick to look at the details. I was impressed to find that it contained both of their names on it, a family crest and underneath their names it said, board members, mentors, and scholarships.

These people were on a different playing field compared to most retired people. They had purpose and identity that went well beyond their work years and roles. And it wasn't like they were crazy wealthy and donating millions of dollars for sport. They were pretty normal people who took a fresh approach to their life in retirement.

The couple not only became clients, but also good personal friends. Taking a cue from them as well as my creative travel clients, I wrote my first book, *Naked Retirement*. It was so named because it was one of the first books to strip out the dollars and cents associated with more traditional planning and begin to help people chart out the non-financial aspects of life in retirement.

Over my 20-year career, I've been fortunate to learn from people who had different perspectives and approaches to life in retirement. One of my favorites was a conversation with a friend who was part of what is often called direct selling, or a network marketing program.

One night, we were out to dinner with a group of friends from church, including her. When my wife and I sat down, we were in a direct conversation path with her. So, I did the unthinkable, I asked a networking marketing person about their business. I was expecting some sort of sales pitch, an offer to try some samples, or an invitation to attend an upcoming rally with their upline. I didn't get any of that.

Instead, I was shocked by what she said. "Well it's not really a business. I do like it and use the company's products so the discounts I get as a distributor are good, but otherwise, I joined the program to keep myself busy and to meet new people."

I was shocked by her response. So much so, that I think I muttered something like, "What do you mean it's not a business and you like it," as I thought to myself, "Where's the lousy sales pitch, samples, and invite?"

She carried on, "Well I started in the business after I was remarried. I was living in a new city and thought going around selling these products would help me meet new people. Also, organizing the orders keeps my mind busy and then moving the boxes and other products around keeps me active. I don't attend all the sales meetings and I don't have parties, I just do a little here and there and it works for us because I get more than a little money out of it."

I was so impressed because this woman found a concrete way to do what my books, articles, and workshops encouraged people to do: Find a way to replace your work identity, and stay relevant and connected as well as mentally and physical active. To her benefit, she had just found it in one place, with a network marketing company rather than piecemealing those things together. It was another eye-opening example of how to approach life in retirement with a fresh and creative design.

In each of the cases above, the assumptions that I made blinded me to the creative side of retirement. Early on with my traveling clients, I assumed they would need a large sum of money to travel, but they had a different plan. One in which they would use their skills and time as currency.

When it came to my retired clients who won the retirement game and had their own business card, I assumed the best way to make a retirement decision was based on what you had saved, rather than a list of 12-15 things you wanted to do after work.

My network marketing friend wasn't bothered by social norms and beliefs about multi-level marketing, she looked beyond the surface, using them to make a successful transition.

Over time, what I have found is that creative retirement planning allows us to stretch our minds, see new and exciting things, and engage ourselves in a way that helps us fulfill our life-long potential. My hope is that you can use these examples and this book to move beyond the traditional retirement planning ideas and assumptions, and instead blaze your own unique path.

About The Author

Robert Laura is the founder of the Retirement Coaches Association and RetirementProject.org. He is the leading voice for the retirement coaching industry and has pioneered many tools and resources to help people prepare for the non-financial aspects of retirement including the Certified Professional Retirement Coach (CPRC) training and designation.

He is the author of several books and guides including *Naked Retirement* and *Retirement Rx*. He is also a nationally syndicated columnist for Forbes.com and *Financial Advisor Magazine*. Robert is a sought-after corporate trainer, speaker, consultant, and financial expert witness. He can be reached at rl@robertlaura.com

Retirement: Insights To Success
And How To Prepare
By Rhonda Fekete

Are you wondering what might be the most important retirement consideration, outside of financial security, to be thinking about before taking the leap? And, speaking of the leap, why do so many of us think of it in this way?

If you're thinking about retiring within one to two years, or if you are already retired and find your situation less than satisfying, these three insider stories offer insights for settling into a richly rewarding retirement.

Go back to the question posited about taking a leap relative to retirement. When I first decided to explore coaching, I discovered the acronym FEAR which stands for *false evidence appearing real*. Seth Godin is quoted as saying, "Anxiety is nothing but repeatedly re-experiencing failure in advance."

We all have fears about something. Retirement doesn't need to be one of those things we fear. Anxiety is created when we allow fear to take over our thoughts. A little bit of planning and thinking ahead can eliminate the *false evidence* that keeps you up at night.

I've written these insider stories because each provides at least one insight to help reduce your fears, foster ideas, generate excitement, and give you courage to move past your fear.

Insider Story No. 1

Jenny and Tom D. retired in 2012 and 2013, respectively. Jenny, a retired second grade teacher, was becoming tired and she knew it was time. Technology was becoming more prevalent and she felt her students could benefit from the next generation of teachers who were better equipped with the necessary technology skills. Consequently, reaching the decision to retire wasn't difficult.

Tom, an executive and owner in a privately owned engineering firm, found his retirement guided by a contractual agreement which stipulated divestiture of stock options by a certain age.

He retired halfway between when he was eligible and when retirement would have been mandated. Let's look at how they are doing today and how each of them have made their respective transitions into retirement.

Prior to Jenny's retirement, she and Tom had discussed where they wanted to live. The neighborhood where they had raised their family was changing and they wanted something new. Jenny's first year of retirement was focused on deciding where to live. Then, she and Tom could become involved in all the activities that would go into building their new home. The end of one journey (her teaching career) became the beginning of another journey (retirement and new home).

While Jenny ventured into retirement without Tom, he was already preparing plans to follow soon thereafter. He announced his retirement approximately three years ahead of the 2013 planned date. This gave him time to transition with his business partners and, with the date in mind, it was just a matter of executing on the plan.

When asked how Tom dealt with the loss of identity from the executive role he'd once held, his answer was very simple: He didn't experience a loss. Because Tom had been planning for almost three years, his "getting ready" occurred over a period of time. Not all retirements involve stock divestitures which essentially force retirement. However, within lies a strategy that can be learned and applied to any retirement with or without such a constraint.

Fast forward to 2019. How has retirement been for them? Jenny became the primary childcare provider for her granddaughter through her first birthday, at which time she entered day care on a part-time basis. Tom and Jenny both agreed this was an amazing experience and they shared how much fun it has been for the two of them. They now have two granddaughters and Jenny continues to provide childcare two days per week for them.

What else keeps Jenny busy? Lots of things, including axe throwing and learning how to make torchon lace by hand. She credits Tom with introducing her to axe throwing. Jenny, in turn, invited a special friend from her lacemaking group to join her in the axe throwing pursuit just for fun.

After listening to Jenny talk about how much fun it was, I'm keeping an open mind to the possibility of trying it myself.

Jenny likes to experience new things and she acts upon her curiosity. A venture to the Ohio State Fair a couple of years ago piqued her curiosity about lacemaking. She is now engaged in torchon lacemaking classes at the Ghillie Center.[1] I saw Jenny's work and it's quite intricate and beautiful. What an amazing experience and sense of accomplishment it must bring.

Modern-day axe throwing, coupled with a craft believed to date back to the 16th century, are just a couple of things that Jenny was curious about and pursued.

When I asked Tom what he envisioned doing when he planned for his retirement, he saw himself volunteering at The Columbus Zoo, though it never materialized. It has yet to happen because his days are filled with things to do and he hasn't had time. For a while, he mentored Ohio State University (OSU) engineering students until he felt it was in their best interest to be mentored by someone actively working in the industry. Tom doesn't plan too far ahead; he just gets up and does whatever needs to be done and he finds he doesn't have any trouble staying busy.

Tom is the president of the homeowners' association (HOA) in my neighborhood and I live right across the street from him. I'm an early riser –

or so I thought. My alarm typically goes off at 5:30 a.m. and the second one at 5:45. The newspaper arrives weekdays somewhere between 5:45 and 6 a.m. Almost every morning, when I open my front door to retrieve the newspaper from the porch, Tom's car is already gone.

Though neighbors, other than occasional conversations while out in the lawn or driveway and at the annual HOA meeting, I would classify myself as an acquaintance with Jenny and Tom and not close friends. Talking with Tom and Jenny for the purpose of writing about their retirement experience gave me the opportunity to be a nosey neighbor and get to know them a little better.

I recalled having mentioned to Tom that I noticed he leaves awfully early every day and I wondered why someone retired would be doing so. He leaves at "o-dark-hundred" for workouts five days each week. I took the opportunity to dig deeper on the subject. Was it a habit he developed post retirement? Tom indicated he has been doing it for a long time. When I asked how long, he replied that I had asked a great question. While Tom was thinking about exactly how long, Jenny answered for him: since 2001.

I picked up on the fact of Jenny's immediate recall of the timing and I asked if there was some significance to the year. It turned out 2001 was the year Tom had a heart attack. I was shocked, to say the least, because Tom appears to me to be like the Energizer Bunny™.

Working out regularly and participating in group exercise is part of what allows him to be so active now – and active he is. Our neighborhood has reserve areas on both sides of the entrance to our gated community. When someone drives up to the gate entrance, that person may notice the flowerbeds on both sides are well maintained and the ravine reserve areas display an array of colors from the goldenrods and purple wildflowers. A stream runs through the reserve and there are deer and the occasional red fox.

Tom, along with a couple of other retired individuals in the neighborhood, volunteered their time – and a lot of it – over at least a year. They cleaned out brush and stabilized the buckeye trees found growing there after clearing out the honeysuckle that had overtaken the reserve. This is just one of the ways Tom gives back to the community. Staying busy is a theme I have been able to observe in Tom every day since I moved to the neighborhood four years ago.

In closing Jenny and Tom's story, if it sounds like all work and no play for Tom, rest assured there is balance. They have a son and a grandson in Arizona and they make a trip there every other month. They also make an annual trip to Hilton Head, South Carolina. This coming September, they are going to Iceland to celebrate an anniversary when they plan to see the aurora borealis. Congratulations, Jenny and Tom!

Insider Story No. 2

Stephen M. retired in 2010 from a nonprofit organization that raises equity capital for elderly low-income housing ventures. Still in the throes of one of the country's deepest recessions, layoffs were contemplated. Just three months into retirement, "Steve" realized he had made a knee-jerk reaction based on an altruistic desire to preserve jobs for younger employees who were in the prime of their careers. He didn't feel they should lose their jobs and believed early retirement might prevent this from happening. Let's learn from Steve's situation and what he did to resolve the situation. We'll meet his wife, Rachel, and learn how she factored into Steve's retirement strategy and where they are today.

Steve and I have worked together over the past 20-plus years at a couple of organizations, but not since 2007 when we went our separate ways. We do, however, attend the same church, where Steve is an active member and ushers regularly. He and Rachel were one of the first couples who came to mind when I thought about what could be learned about retirement planning through real-life scenarios. Why? Because listening to them share about all their travel plans, I wanted to know how they manage to do this so well.

After realizing the mistake he'd made in retiring too soon, and faced with Rachel being three years from her own retirement, Steve happened to be talking with his former employer. When asked how retirement was going, he replied, "Not so well." His former employer asked if he would be interested in coming back to work. Steve agreed to return on a part-time basis – 32 hours per week instead of 40 hours. He worked for approximately three more years. During this time, Steve and Rachel committed to living off her income as a teacher. Steve's salary was stashed away for retirement – savings of approximately three years' worth.

Note: Although this book is not intended to focus on the financial aspects of retirement, it's important that Steve emphasized the amount of time and number of extensive budgets he prepared to determine what they needed to do to prepare for their desired version of retirement.

Steve and Rachel both love history and they began making a list of all the places they wanted to travel in retirement. They have sons who live out of state and a grandchild they knew they would want to visit often – a factor in planning for travel expenses.

Just to provide perspective on what is possible with planning, I will list some of the places they have travelled (including seven Viking River Cruises, and various Mediterranean and Balkan Islands).

- China
- Croatia
- Europe
- France
- Istanbul, Turkey
- Italy

- Portugal
- Russia
- Spain
- United Kingdom

I laughed when Steve commented that he and Rachel are some of the younger people in their tour groups. Most of the travelers are in their 80s – another reason that taking care of your physical well-being is so important to a fulfilling retirement. I commented that I've never been a fan of tour groups – bus-tour groups specifically – but Steve insists it is the way to go.

My curiosity wondered what Steve and Rachel do when they are not traveling. Steve estimated that he has completed between 22-26 courses through The Ohio State University's Program 60, which offers tuition-free, non-credit/non-degree programs.[2] Steve's courses have focused on history or anthropology. Many colleges and universities across the country offer similar programs, if you are wondering how you might fill some of your time in retirement.

While Steve spends some of his free time auditing classes, Rachel likes to volunteer her time working with their church's refugee relief program. As you can see, giving back is an important part of both of their lives. Steve commented he knows they have been very blessed and he's very grateful for all they have and are able to do. It is widely known that research reveals the benefits of practicing gratitude on overall well-being. Steve and Rachel demonstrate this so well.

When I asked Steve what he'd do differently if he had it to do over again, of course, he wouldn't have retired the first time. He acted on impulse versus having a well-thought-out retirement strategy. His advice to others: Practice living off one income before retirement to see how it feels and to get used to what it will be like. And to quote Steve, "It really is all about planning and being realistic about what your income will allow you to do."

Insider Story No. 3

Jan T. engaged in a retirement coaching engagement with me because she was thinking about retirement but had not yet pulled the trigger due to a degree of uncertainty. Jan is single, has an adult son, and finds herself in an organization where she is no longer interested in working beyond retirement eligibility. She feels financially ready, but there was still some hesitation about making the formal commitment to retire. Jan's story details how retirement coaching helped to provide clarity and solidify her decision to retire at the beginning of 2020.

During my initial coaching session with Jan, what appeared to resonate most with her was when we talked about her idea of spending an extended vacation in Tuscany. She knew with certainty, the first six months of retirement would be reserved for nothing – meaning nothing that required planning (a bit of a reward, if you will) for all the years leading up to this event.

My coaching philosophy believes the client does the work, including identifying the focus of each coaching session. Thus, Jan would spend the following week researching and planning her trip to Tuscany.

When we met a week later, Jan shared vividly who she would travel with, the months she would travel, and for how long. Her friend would join her for two weeks and her son for another two weeks. Afterward, she envisioned spending the second month immersing herself in a small Tuscan neighborhood getting to know the locals and learning as much as she could about their way of life. I was beginning to sense Jan becoming more confident in her decision to retire. (Listening to Jan, I was becoming excited about possibly planning my own trip to Tuscany where my husband would love to go!)

Jan's life journey was inspired by a friend who convinced her to move to San Francisco where she spent 10 years before returning to Columbus. She spoke of it being a time in her life when she was with someone who loved adventure. She was introduced to doing things she never would have done on her own.

I smile as I think of the influence on Jan's ability to plan for a trip to Tuscany as a single woman. She shared stories about her friends from college with whom she remains close, regular dates for playing bridge, and travel to Washington, DC, during cherry blossom season. Museums play heavily in her travels.

She spoke of doing volunteer work, though she hasn't quite landed on exactly what type of volunteering she will do. She loves working with youth, so maybe something in this realm. She's been an inspiration to younger co-workers, whose paths crossed with hers and who later shared the impact she had on them. This is a gift and one I know she will find a way to use in retirement.

What is your dream retirement? How big can you envision and with what level of detail? What's holding you back from making these plans right now?

Key Take-Aways

I wanted to know what Jenny, Tom, Steve, and Jan had learned from retirement – and planning for retirement – they could share with others.

Jenny and Tom

- Jenny was noticeably emotional when I asked what surprised her about retirement. She responded how important friends are in retirement and, particularly, female friends. Maintaining friends from the past, but making new friends through new experiences has been very rewarding for her, along with getting curious and trying new things.

- Tom's strategy for easing into retirement over an extended timeframe prepared him mentally for the day that would eventually come. How can you begin preparing yourself to do the same, whether you are forced into retirement, or you do so by choice?
- Tom's focus on his physical well-being and exercise is a critical factor for an enjoyable retirement. Recall, too, the habit began long before Tom's retirement date. Build habits now so you can carry them into retirement instead of waiting for when you will have more time. The time is now. You'll be so much happier because you will be active and energetic. Do not allow physical limitations to dampen the things you dream of doing in retirement. Get active before you retire and stay active!

Stephen M.

- Steve's message is to avoid making a knee-jerk reaction to retire without first thinking it through and planning. Steve had the luxury of returning to a job he enjoyed for another three years before officially retiring the second time. Living off one income after the initial misstep of retiring too soon made travel, to the extent they wanted to travel, a reality. If you have already experienced a similar retirement misstep, what can you do to re-engage in work you are passionate about?
- Engage your brain regularly. Steve's auditing of college-level classes is a great way to continue learning while interacting with younger

generations – an added benefit that keeps you feeling more youthful.

- Count your blessings through gratitude. Being thankful for your health, friends, and what you have (versus thinking about what you do not have) is an invaluable resource and costs you nothing.

Jan T.

Jan T. gave thoughtful consideration to whether she should retire and, if so, when? Such trepidation is not uncommon. By putting some thought and planning (through retirement coaching) into how she'd spend her first year of retirement, Jan became more excited and settled into making retirement her soon-to-be reality. She now has a timeframe for retiring and she is looking forward to when she will make the formal announcement to her employer.

- A subtle take-away from Jan's story is that of being single and retiring. At no time did Jan mention the fact she is single and how this might impact her retirement. Her strong network of friends plays heavily into what she looks forward to in her retirement. A theme we saw, that Jenny identified, as being a critical factor for a rewarding retirement.
- A quote from Jan may say it best about the benefits of Retirement Coaching: "As I plan to retire in the next year, I will think more about what to do with my time and not only plan financially. I will work toward learning and

volunteering in a more focused manner. It never really occurred to me to plan my time and create goals for myself in retirement. It was fun and eye opening to think of things in a new way. I am more confident in my retirement plan."

Conclusion

What is the most important retirement consideration you should be thinking about? The stories, just shared, of real-life situations show us there is no one-size-fits-all answer to this question. Retirement is an individual adventure which is yours to design and then to live.

What do you want to do in retirement – literally – every day and throughout the weeks to come? Where do you want to live in retirement? More importantly, assuming your finances are in order, what is the fear that is holding you back?

When considering what you will do once retired, don't overlook the theme which appeared in each of the insight stories shared; volunteering. Society is in great need of the skills, knowledge, and experience Baby Boomers have to offer. What a wonderful legacy to leave from your life's third chapter by giving back in a meaningful way and contributes toward the benefit of others.

Get started on creating your retirement plans now. Put your pen to paper and start building your plans. Make retirement all that you can dream possible! And, if you need some help, locate a certified professional retirement coach to support you in designing your retirement journey.

About The Author

Rhonda Fekete works for a Fortune 100 financial services firm based in Columbus, Ohio. She coaches internal and field sales leaders and facilitates coach training and development programs. She holds an MBA from Franklin University and a master's degree in professional practice in coaching from Middlesex University (London, UK). She is an associated certified coach (ACC/ICF) and certified master business coach (CMBC/WABC), as well as a member of the International Coach Federation. Formerly, she was financial controller and HR leader at PricewaterhouseCoopers, CAO and HR Director for an industry-leading public finance firm, and served in legal industry HR director roles. She most recently completed the certified professional retirement coach designation through RetirementProject.org. Contact Rhonda at consult@careerpointeconsulting.com

Notes

[1] Torchon Lace Making at the Ghillie Center, https://www.columbusunderground.com/lacemakers -of-central-ohio-uphold-centuries-old-craft-rw1

[2] The Ohio State University Program 60 ttps://program60.osu.edu/

This Wasn't The Retirement We Planned
By Drummond Osborn

A quick flip through popular magazines or a slow surf through social media presents Madison Avenue's view of retirement – perfectly coifed, silver hairs on the happy heads of a healthy couple strolling the beach at sunset. For some – such as the models in those pictures – that might be a retirement reality. But for most others, it's a different reality. Allow me to introduce Millie and Paul.

They had met early in their working careers, Millie was providing clerical services at the local hospital and Paul was a clinical psychologist. A chance passing glance in a back hallway was all it took to ignite the romance for a lifetime. Never one to date a co-worker, Paul's knowingly short stint at the hospital was followed by a quick call to Millie. And as they say, the rest became history.

That history included several years of dating before what friends recognized was an inevitable marriage. Millie remained at the hospital, advancing through the organization to positions of increased responsibility. Paul's small private practice grew to a size that allowed for a nice balance between personal and professional life.

It wasn't long before his control over scheduling allowed him to fill the role of "Mr. Mom" while their children were young. Later, he would integrate that flexibility into the household schedule as school filled the days for their kids. Millie continued full-time employment at the hospital. Her many years on staff allowed her to nibble at the beginning and end of her workdays to be very present and involved with the kids.

A simple cabin in the nearby woods was a regular focus of retirement-related conversations, typically, over cups of coffee and chai tea in the quiet of early Sunday mornings. Though the children soon grew and built their own lives, the cabin has yet to be built. A slow-moving illness took Paul's life before retirement.

Few individuals are ever prepared for the turn of the page which leads to an abrupt flip into the next chapter. Couples instinctively know that solo retirement, for one of them, is on the horizon. But typically, that horizon is seen as hosting a near endless series of sunrises and sunsets. Millie and Paul hadn't really thought about a 60-something solo-retirement, but upon reflection the way they lived their lives provided Millie with the sketch of a blueprint.

Independent Teamwork

Far from being social butterflies, Mille and Paul did enjoy the social interactions that were woven into their places of work. Millie's career had taken her to the executive suite at the same hospital where she and Paul had met. There, she handled the administrative assistant responsibilities for the human resource director. As one of the hospital's long-term employees, she knew most of the staff and had developed friendships with employees, old and new.

Friendships transcended work hours, as Millie had regular, bi-monthly post-work pizza with several co-workers. The get-togethers originally coincided with paydays. And though pay-cycles and participants changed over the many years, the ritual remained.

Paul's work setting was very different, as a bare-bones staff supported just a couple of professionals. His human interaction was mostly on a professional level with patients, but was none-the-less an important, energizing part of his workday.

Like Millie, his non-patient work relationships continued outside of the office, as he and the other psychologists were part of a cycling club. When calendars aligned, Millie and Paul would vacation with some neighborhood friends. What began as a series of frenzied trips with kids, continued as calmer vacations to a rented cabin in the woods.

Though not viewed as an intentional piece of their retirement plan, Millie and Paul had established supportive social structures – individually and together. Before Paul's death, and throughout his prolonged illness, there was a social structure, both at work and outside work, with common friends and experiences, as well as relationships and activities which were separate and independent.

Just A Dash Of Money

Financial stress was never part of any equation for Millie and Paul. They had always ascribed to a "save-then-spend" approach to life. Neither of them had chased high-paying careers. So, even before two households became one, each of them lived well within their single-life means. Joining those habits and attitudes under one roof worked well as they moved through the stages of life from newlyweds to busy parents and then to empty nesters.

Though never considered financially affluent by income earned nor assets accumulated, they relied on professional advisors to help keep them on track – an attorney for their wills, a longtime agent for their insurance, and a broker for their investments. Attention to the fine details was a well-honed workplace skill, but their own financial plans were made up of generalities.

They didn't have a specific goal for the size of their nest egg, because regular saving, Millie's small pension, and a controlled-spending lifestyle had them feeling blindly comfortable about their future. There was also no specific retirement date circled on their calendar, just a reference to "sometime."

Millie quietly had one eye on age 62 as a possible retirement starting point. By then, she would have completed a seeming milestone of 40 years at the hospital. Paul on the other, couldn't imagine completely giving up his patients. He could, however, clearly envision a small panel of patients allowing for a modest number of office hours, with maximum flexibility.

Their save-then-spend approach to life did have one bump in the road – the kids. Higher education had provided Millie and Paul with opportunities for satisfying careers, and they wanted the same for their children. Paul's stay-at-home parenting did come with the price of reduced household income.

So, saving for college, on one-and-one-half incomes, didn't fit their budget as nicely as they had hoped. Instead, they agreed to fund college for their children with a combination of savings and loans. Once the kids were in college, they agreed Paul could ramp up his practice a bit, paying off any debt already accumulated and cash-flowing the rest. The kids would graduate debt free, while Millie and Paul would certainly have those loans paid off before their own graduation into retirement. This part of their life seemed well planned. Unfortunately, Paul's health didn't allow him to ramp up his practice the way they had hoped, and some of the debt remained.

Time To Retire

A couple years prior to Paul's passing, Millie began to hone in on retirement at age 62. She still enjoyed her co-workers, but she no longer felt energized by her time at work. Paul was having good days and not-so-good days, and an early retirement would allow them to enjoy the good days all the more.

But that plan was not to be. Paul died before Millie retired. She had, however, accrued enough time off to get her close to her official 40th work anniversary. So, she quietly submitted her retirement notification.

One might view this as a sad tale of retirement lost, but for Millie that wasn't the case. Though she would never characterize retirement without Paul as easy, she was ready to move into this next phase of life – a phase, which for Millie, was supported by a framework quietly built over many years.

Retirement had never been planned as being some new, idyllic adventure. It was always seen as a simple transition away from a 40-hour, work-a-day life to an opportunity for spending those former work hours in already familiar ways.

For some, a bit of introspection reveals the underpinnings for a successful transition to a post-paycheck lifestyle, while others may require a light to be shone on this framework, by others. In the context of a brief chapter, only a quick sketch of Millie has been provided. So, below are some highlights, and some new details, that allowed for Millie's seemingly solo venture into retirement.

Social Well-Being

Two distinct supportive social circles had been developed and nurtured over the years. One included Paul, and one had not. Both circles, however, provided connectedness and continuity as Millie entered retirement.

Neighborhood friends knew Millie, primarily, as part of Millie and Paul. Her pizza-payday friends knew Millie as an individual, as opposed to being part of a couple. Her retirement calendar continues to intentionally include both.

For your consideration: Whether retirement is years down the road, or suddenly upon you, acknowledge, embrace, and expand the social circles around you. Social circles which exist independently of one another provide an aspect of autonomy, allowing one relationship circle to be supportive while another might struggle or disappear completely.

Some added info: Millie's vision for a retirement cabin in the woods was born of her love for nature. In addition to all other things, the setting served as her muse for writing. Millie is still in the early stages of her retirement, and though she has no cabin porch upon which to sit and write, walks through those woods seem to motivate her pen just as easily.

Keeping Finances In Their Place

Finances are certainly a part of the equation for retirement success, but Millie and Paul proved money wasn't *the* focus. Financial success, for them, was more accurately about financial independence. And financial independence was simply an ability to no longer depend on full-time employment.

The equation began with saving regularly and spending less, which added up to control and success. Millie was certainly no spendthrift, nor was she a penny pincher. She maintained a healthy outlook toward spending that always recognized she couldn't spend what she didn't have.

For your consideration: High finance begins with basic math, and that math simply requires some savings before any spending. The result is a growing nest egg and a control over spending. These are habits and attitudes which are never too late to adopt.

Some added information: Retirement was never seen as an all or nothing venture, as Paul had intended to continue receiving some income by working with at least a few patients.

Millie's position at the hospital didn't allow for such flexibility, but her love for writing in, and about, nature allowed her to do some freelance writing during the hours she used to spend at work. She currently earns a few extra dollars submitting short articles to publications in her area, and directs most of that income toward the debt she still carries.

A Purpose-Filled Future

Healthy living (even with the occasional pizza on paydays) was part of who Millie and Paul had always been. Paul played out that passion in his role as a mental health professional and a cyclist. While Millie's professional skills could have transferred to most any organization, she loved working in a healthcare organization.

The retirement cabin in the woods was, again, not just a place to hang their hats, but was an embodiment of a healthy, outdoors lifestyle. That was part of Millie's basic fabric. A lack of her own cabin in the woods wasn't enough to derail this passion. Finding ways to maintain this connection throughout the various phases and stages of life provided familiarity as Millie transitioned into retirement.

For your consideration: Recognizing one's passion and purpose isn't always as easy as some might think. A lifetime of activities and interests may become so routine that they might not be labeled as a passion, yet they are.

- What settings provide you with energy and excitement?
- Are there activities that consistently reappear on your calendar, year after year?
- Do your spending habits or charitable contributions point to a certain interest?

Retirement success can be built on allocating more time to what is already a passion. But just as there is healthy support to be found through social circles which aren't always connected, it is equally important to avoid letting any single passion become too all encompassing.

Some additional info: Millie's passion and purpose at the hospital allowed her to forego ever setting a morning alarm. She was excited to jump out of bed every day – until she wasn't. This was a key contributor to her early retirement. But with skills that easily transferred, a motivation that was driven by purpose over pennies, she sought and found a part-time clerical position with a local health-related nonprofit.

About The Author

At an early age the author recognized his passion for all things financial, and soon thereafter understood how that passion was inseparable from his need for helping others. Today, Drummond Osborn, CFP®, RICP®, operates a small wealth-advisory business, located in Northwest Indiana, focused on redefining the Madison-Avenue-image of retirement by helping the Millies and Pauls of the world find success in a passion-filled, post-paycheck phase of life. In addition to working with new clients, he is always interested in hearing stories that help redefine retirement. He'd welcome hearing from you at ddo@OsbornWealthManagement.com.

Dr. Janet McNeill Hively: A 21st Century Hero
By Dorian Mintzer

People have said that there aren't role models for retirement in the 21st century. I disagree. There are "heroes" hiding in plain sight. They are pathfinders, or "wayshowers" we can look to and learn from. In this chapter, I'll focus on Dr. Jan Hively, a pioneer in the positive aging movement and exemplar of positive, successful, productive and creative aging.

You probably haven't heard the term "wayshower." I hadn't either, until I read a wonderful book by Olivia Ames Hoblitzelle, called *Aging with Wisdom: Reflections, Stories, and Teachings*. Hobitzelle comments that she isn't sure when she first heard the term, but likes it, and so do I.

Often, people tell others what they should be doing or how they should be living their lives. Wayshowers, in contrast, do things in their own way, and become role models for others who are inspired to do it similarly or to find their own way. Jan, as a colleague and now dear friend, has been a wayshower – showing ways to age while she continues to grow, embrace life, and give back to help make the world better for future generations.

I met Jan at the first Positive Aging Conference in 2007. She was influenced as a teenager by the writings of John Stuart Mill on utilitarianism. Much of her life and work has involved figuring out what will make the greatest positive impact and what is likely to be the cost-benefit ratio of the impact.

In other words, when she considers what she wants to do about a significant issue, Jan asks, "What can I do that will make the biggest positive difference?" She has continued to reinvent herself as she has aged, developing programs that impact and connect people locally as well as globally.

The First 50 Years

Jan was born in January 1932, and now has 88 years of life experiences. She has had to deal with many life challenges (internal and external), and evidences grit, resilience, grace, and gratitude. She personifies an elder who values her own life and contributions, learns with and from others (younger and older), and lives her mantra: "Meaningful work, paid or unpaid, through one's last breath."

She grew up in Arlington, Massachusetts, Portland, Maine, and Hartford, Connecticut. Her father was a widower with two children when he married Jan's mother. Her sister, with whom she is still very close, is 10 years older (now with 98 years of life experience) and her brother is seven years older (now 95 years of life experience).

There are longevity genes in her generation! Her father died after a long illness when she was 16 years old and her mother supported the family. She didn't have playmates her own age and relied on her own self, intellect, and love of reading and learning.

Jan was an independent and spunky person. She describes how when she was 13, she filled out her own application, signed her parents' names, and got herself admitted to an excellent private girls' school where she studied a lot more than the basics, including philosophy. She later was admitted with a scholarship to Radcliffe College in Harvard University.

Her life was derailed when she developed polio at age 19. Although she was told by her doctors that she'd have to use braces to walk, they were never needed. Luckily for Jan, she had some former Marine nurses who had been trained by Sister Elizabeth Kenny in Australia to work with polio victims. They set up a pulley system over her hospital bed so she could exercise her limbs.

By the next year, she was able to walk (albeit with a limp and drop-foot) and ride her bicycle, and she pledged to be grateful all her life for her recovery. She returned to Radcliffe to finish her undergraduate degree. Her boyfriend/future husband, who had also contracted polio in his right arm and shoulder, had visited her daily once he had recovered.

Jan wanted to marry, to move out of her mother's home, and become independent. She was a product of the times. She worked on army bases while her husband served in the Korean War, and worked in textbook editing while he completed his Ph.D.

Then, for 8 years, she enjoyed life as a faculty wife raising two children and engaged as a community activist. When she was 40, however, her husband told her he didn't love her and wanted, instead, to be with a colleague. She went through a devastating divorce and found herself on her own with only part-time child custody.

Evidencing her survival instincts and resilience, she utilized some of her contacts in her volunteer networks and found nourishing jobs that focused on her community interests in education, environmental quality, and community planning and completed a master's degree with evening classes.

Jan got married again, to a friend of the family who was 22 years older and chaired the University of Minnesota Psychology Department. She described him as her best friend, teacher, and career counselor who offered much-needed "unconditional love."

Community Support For Child/Youth Development

Jan worked her way up through positions in city, metropolitan and school district planning. She served as deputy mayor for Minneapolis through the 1980s. Working through the mayor's office, she was able to foster broad-based community collaboration on programs supporting child and youth development from pre-birth through to adulthood. A few of the programs, including Success by Six, the

Buddy System, Career Beginnings, and the Youth Coordinating Board developed as national models.

Then and now, Jan is interested in how we teach and learn the skills, habits and attitudes that are basic to productivity. With support from the McKnight Foundation, Jan left the mayor's office in 1989 to develop her first nonprofit organization, Youth Trust, engaging public/private/nonprofit employers in school-business partnerships that generated "Work-ready youth for a youth-ready workplace." Youth Trust programs encouraged experiential learning related to productivity.

The Youth Trust is now called Achieve Minneapolis, with employers investing mentoring time and dollars to staff a technology guidance lab in every high school and a process for every student to develop a career portfolio.

After the deaths of her mother and husband, Jan moved from Minneapolis to Chicago in 1991 as president of the Golden Apple Foundation, expanding its programs for excellence in teaching statewide, and helping to start two programs with the Chicago Schools: Future Teachers, and Teachers for Chicago.

She returned to Minneapolis in 1994 as director of statewide outreach for the University of Minnesota College of Education and Human Development. In that role, she wrote the state's manual for School to Work programming that integrated classroom learning with community service learning and workplace learning. She then worked statewide to encourage all students to start Lifework Planning as early as elementary school.

The process called for students to set regular goals for their learning both inside and outside the classroom, to report on their goal achievements at parent-student-teacher conferences, and to receive feedback from their parents and teachers before setting goals for the next round. As always, she stressed the importance of experiential learning to the primary goal of education – preparing independent, self-guided learners.

Positive Aging Advocacy Networks

By taking classes as well as working, Jan completed her Ph.D. in 2001 at age 69. She was drawn by concern about the plight of older adults in rapidly aging rural communities from which young adults had migrated to the cities. But her surveys revealed the extraordinary productivity of older adults who, when compared with those in cities, were employed longer, volunteered more, and provided care for friends and neighbors as well as family.

On average, 75% of those from ages 55-84 described themselves as healthy, active, and feeling relatively happy and in control of life. Her surprising discoveries changed her own ageist perceptions and led her to create the Minnesota Vital Aging Network through the University of Minnesota that:

- Raised awareness about the potential for positive, productive aging lifelong
- Helped older adults find pathways to build on their strengths
- Advocated for Vital Communities that support positive aging.

Jan talks about the decade of her 70s as the best years of her life. She received a major grant in 2005 to sustain the Vital Aging Network, which is still thriving. She helped develop one of the offshoots created by its members, the Minnesota Creative Arts and Aging Network, now called ArtSage. The goal of that group was to stimulate the active creative expression of every older adult through programs developed by professional artists, because research has tied the power of creative expression to healthy, positive aging.

In 2007, Jan co-founded the SHIFT Network as a grassroots community of people in midlife and beyond who were seeking meaningful work. Meeting in coffeehouses, with social interaction along with presentations, adults who had been laid off along with others who were looking for post-retirement options found a way to share their stories and talk about "what's next." Jan talks about finding community for herself as well as for others through SHIFT, which now has professional staff and a stable meeting place for large group forums, complemented by regular small group meetings in coffee houses around the region.

Jan has been active with the growth of several national networks fostering older adult development, including the Life Planning Network, Encore.org, and the Positive Aging movement. Beginning in 2009, she's been working with Moira Allan, a life coach in Paris, to create an international network of positive aging advocates.

Through World Café Europe, they were funded to organize World Cafés in six European countries to connect civic leaders and older adults in conversations about positive aging for the European Union's Year of Active Ageing, 2012. The conversations generated so much interest that Moira and Jan launched the global Pass It On Network in 2013 with a website (www.passitonnetwork.org) and a monthly newsletter.

Now, the Pass It On Network has over 70 country liaisons around the globe. Without external funding, she and Moira have created a worldwide digital community that is a robust and thriving organization, enabling positive aging advocates to "pass on" their knowledge and programs to each other so no one has to "reinvent the wheel."

Thanks to Zoom, the liaisons can meet and collaborate. Some also travel and meet in person. For example, five liaisons (from Canada, the United States, Nigeria, India, and Malawi) represented Pass It On at a recent meeting of the United Nations Working Group on Ageing in New York City.

Jan moved from Minnesota to Cape Cod in 2010 to be near and help her two aging cousins. She took her energy, insight, and advocacy to her new home, and is happy to travel via the Internet rather than by airplane. She enjoys introducing people around the world who share common interests.

She says, "The future is in peer-to-peer networks, not in traditional, hierarchical organizations. Innovative ideas flow like electricity through our networks, collecting resources from nodes along the way so they can adapt and evolve – just like life itself."

Teaching/Learning Together

Wherever she is, Jan loves to share thoughts with people in small groups. For the past four years we have both belonged to a Wisdom Circle in the Boston area where we explore "ageing and sage-ing" in our society. Jan has now begun a Wisdom Circle in her Cape Cod community.

She's developed programs helping her town of Yarmouth to become an Age Friendly Community. She's helped plan intergenerational Model United Nation programs that pair high school students with elders to discuss international issues such as water, ageing, and women's rights.

Jan has successfully promoted a local ban on town distribution or sale of single-use plastic beverage bottles. She views it as an important consciousness-raising process to get people started toward making the dramatic changes that will be required to achieve sustainable development goals.

She believes we are teachers and learners all our lives. The purpose of education for young people is to cultivate enthusiastic, independent learners who are curious to learn more. She views the primary purpose of higher education as teaching people to think like researchers – to create a hypothesis, try it out, and see if it works.

If it doesn't work, to try a different hypothesis until you discover what does work, and then teach it as a model. What works, what fits? She's a process person, constantly looking for ways of dealing with common issues so that Pass It On can spread the information around and so positive aging advocates can apply the process to meet their local needs.

Jan sees that the biggest challenge in the field of ageing is changing the mindset of older adults who are accustomed to being passive consumers waiting for the next service to be delivered. Extended longevity, combined with climate change and new technologies, requires every one of us to think, and act, like an advocacy leader.

She has co-developed two advocacy leadership training programs: Advocacy Leadership for Vital Aging, now called EVOLVE, offered through the Vital Aging Network; and ALPA, Advocacy Leadership for Positive Aging, offered through the Life Planning Network for providers of aging services to see themselves as advocacy leaders for themselves and their clients.

Jan's life and work illustrates the importance of connection, engagement, purpose, and meaning as the foundation for well-being. In addition to her work, her life illustrates the importance of love and meaningful relationships throughout life.

She and her partner, Tom, who is 12 years her junior, have celebrated 27 years of a life partnership. They share love for each other and a passion for living fully and for lifelong learning. Similarly, Jan's relationships with her daughter, Kate, and son, Dean, are close and rich although Kate lives in Seattle and Dean in Washington, DC. The three of them go on a week's retreat each year to integrate new experiences and old memories as best friends.

Dr. Jan Hively is a hero, role model and wayshower for aging with vitality and dignity. Living life fully as we age has both challenges and opportunities. Jan is a wonderful, wise woman and elder with an amazing mind and spirit. She believes in a life-work-planning emphasis throughout life and in education, where learning occurs at home, in school, in the workplace, and in the community.

The underlying questions for her are, "Will what I do be helpful and useful now and in the future?" and "If not, how do I change it, so it is helpful?" She has been developing her legacy throughout her life, through the amazing programs she's developed and her wonderful friendships and relationships. For her, it's all about making and developing connections. I feel blessed to be a friend and colleague and part of her life.

She has been a wayshower for me—showing me the way to positive, successful, productive and creative aging which includes gratitude, forgiveness, realistic optimism, resilience, acceptance, and transcendence. She is living up to her mantra: "Meaningful work, paid or unpaid, through one's last breath." Thank you, Jan, for being part of my life and a wayshower for so many people.

About The Author

Dr. Dorian "Dori" Mintzer, an experienced speaker, coach, therapist and consultant, weaves adult development, holistic life planning and positive psychology into programs that tap and shape clients' energies into roadmaps for wiser, more enhanced living. She is co-author of *The Couples Retirement Puzzle: 10 Must-Have Conversations for Creating an Amazing New Life Together,* co-producer of *The Career Playbook: Second Half Plays* and has contributed to other books. She is host of the popular monthly Revolutionize your Retirement Interviews with Experts Series.

She's been featured in a variety of media including the *New York Times*, *Wall Street Journal*, *USA Today*, CNN Money, *Forbes.com*, NPR, *ABC Evening News*, and the *Today Show*. She's given a

Ted X talk: "Embracing your Bonus Years." Learn more about Dori at www.revolutionizeretirement.com or dorian@dorianmintzer.com

Resources

Olivia Ames Hoblitzelle, *Aging with Wisdom: Reflections, Stories and Teachings* (Rhinebeck, NY: Monkfish Book Publishing, 2017).

Women and Retirement:
The À La Carte Approach
By Virginia Macali

In a restaurant, you can order a set meal or you can put together your own à la carte menu, where you choose what's most delicious, enjoyable, and satisfying to you. The same may be said of retirement. Each person's life, perspective, and direction dictate what is on the retirement menu of activities, relationships, and opportunities.

Here are stories from five women that detail their à la carte retirement menus. These stories illustrate how women transitioned into retirement and how they are living their lives now. They show choices, activities, perspective, lessons learned, and hints at what's next.

You'll see themes in these stories:

1. Lifelong values and interests continue and amplify in retirement.
2. Commitment to friendships and relationships deepens.
3. Flexibility and willingness to change create opportunities.
4. Time and freedom allow for travel, creativity, and volunteering.
5. Realistic optimism about the future is illuminated.

Easy Going Active Retirement

Jean's à la carte retirement menu includes service, relationships, community, designing a new home, travel, culture, art, and volunteering.

Jean, 71, had a career in a variety of roles in Peace Corps, VISTA, and other nonprofit organizations. All these roles centered around service, a key value and purpose in her life.

While in mid-career phase, Jean had to leave Peace Corps due to a rule that ended employment after five years. She enjoyed this work so much that she wondered who she would be without that identity. She surprised herself by finding the transition a smooth one. Attending graduate school in organizational development helped with the shift; this led to the opportunity to train and develop people in nonprofit organizations. Jean credits that transition as helping her, years later, shift into retirement without fear.

After years of consulting, Jean had the opportunity to work and serve again in countries throughout the world. Later, she did part-time flexible consulting work where she interviewed people pursuing work overseas. This gave her the opportunity to talk to amazing people doing great things in the world.

When she officially retired, she was not as attached to her career identity as she thought she would be. Her first focus was to design and build a new house in a small, summer resort community where family members also had homes. From design to decorating, she expressed her creativity.

Jean sold her home in a large city. She loves to entertain in her new home and invites friends from near and far. These visits provide time for satisfying conversations, sharing mutual interests, and deepening friendships. To get involved locally, Jean plays bridge, volunteers at hospice, and serves on the board of an arts organization.

While she enjoys the simple lifestyle and beauty of nature in this small town, she knew she also wanted to visit larger cities and travel the world for new experiences, culture, and inspiration.

She plans to take one international trip each year for the first five years of retirement. Each winter she travels to visit friends and goes on a jazz cruise to enjoy her favorite music.

Jean is enjoying leisure and having unstructured time. She thinks it is important to have a retirement that matches your personality type. As an easy-going person, she enjoys an easy-going retirement.

She is not worried about older age, although she knows things change and she will have to figure things out. She wonders what that time of life will be like, what she'll need, and what she will do.

Jean ticks off what's important to her in retirement and life: relationships, community, service, travel and culture. She says, "This is a time for me to have more of those things in my life."

When thinking about the future, Jean dreams of sharing a home with friends for fun, camaraderie, and creativity.

Lessons learned: Pay attention to what brings you joy and pleasure and take the steps to make it happen.

The First Six Months

Amy's à la carte retirement menu includes friends, family, travel, home renovation, puppy, creativity, being a stay-at-home mom, and volunteering.

Amy, 61, was an administrator in business operations for a major urban school district throughout her career. She describes her job as demanding and stressful. Six months into retirement, she says, "The big thing for me is that I don't want to jump in and volunteer for a lot right now."

Amy became a parent later in life, which, along with her career, left little or no time for friends or leisure activities. Priorities in her first year of retirement remedy this. She is re-connecting and having reunions with friends she has not been in touch with for many years. She travels and attends beading retreats where she expresses her artistic side. This was one leisure activity that she engaged in while she was working. She looks forward to spending more time with this passion now that she's retired.

One year away from being an empty nester, Amy's relishing being a stay-at-home-mom. She is undertaking a major home renovation and enjoying the antics of her new puppy. On the volunteer front, Amy is using her administrative skills to start a parent booster organization at her son's school.

What's ahead? Within the next few months, Amy will look for part-time paid work so she can add to her discretionary income. She's excited to choose work she can do where money is not the driver. She would like to volunteer in hospice since that organization provided so much comfort to her and her family in the past.

Lessons learned: In the early months of retirement, remember not to take on everything at once. It's helpful to set daily or weekly goals to stay on track.

Flexibility And Shifts

Marcie's à la carte retirement menu includes semi-retirement with a family focus, having an empty nest, serving as a board member, volunteering, consulting, and self-development; going back to work in a leadership role, developing a work-life balance, and finding flexibility and ease; a current retirement with gifts, engagement, and discovery.

Marcie, 67, entered her first retirement after 30 years in public administration and human services. She thought she might work again at some point, but she was unsure whether it would be full time. This semi-retirement lasted five years.

The first year, she planned to do nothing for payment. Instead, she focused on her family and served on boards that reflected her interests and passions in the community. She did not accept any full-time work or long-term commitments.

Part of Marcie's motivation for retiring was to have more time to raise her daughter during her teen years. She drove her daughter and her friends to school and took them on summer trips. None of this would have happened if she stayed in her all-consuming public position.

As her daughter entered her later high school years and was more independent, Marcie was ready to take on more commitments. She travelled to do consulting work the last year of her semi-retirement, and that's how she was drawn to be a leader for an organization rather than continuing in strategic planning.

In what Chris Farrell names *unretirement*,[1] Marcie went back to work. She moved into a leadership position in a community-based organization. She enjoyed this role, where she experienced better work-life balance. After four and a half years in this role, she transitioned to her current retirement.

Now, Marcie is happy that she's not working. She longs to have her gifts brought more into the world and to engage in new ways. She looks forward to discovering more about herself and life during this adventure.

Lessons learned: Know where you are in life. If you are considering going back to work, don't rush into something. Consider whether your reasons for retirement have shifted due to changes in family, finances or other factors. Find and pursue what is meaningful to you.

Phasing Out And Phasing In

Linda's à la carte retirement menu includes celebration, passion, purpose, yoga, and spaciousness.

Linda, 59, was an elementary school teacher for 16 years before she transitioned to a career of marketing and product management for an educational publishing company. For 12 years, she travelled extensively in what she describes as busy, hectic, and crazy work.

Following a corporate re-organization, Linda became part of a new start-up within the company. She saw this as the turning point where she could make a career change. She negotiated a phase-out from corporate work and toward retirement.

In the phase-out, Linda works 3-10 hours a week, which allows time for teaching yoga. Over the past several years, she has pursued her passion of yoga as she enrolled in teacher training and became a certified yoga teacher.

Once she had these tools, she didn't have time to do anything with them since she was working full time. The phase-out gives her the opportunity to phase-in teaching yoga to people of all ages.

Linda's aware that she is not completely detached yet from her work. She is thinking about the question, "How do we make retirement feel like a celebration and the start to something new?" She now sees that she didn't take the time and space to reflect on the ending of her earlier teaching career.

In her words, it just fizzled away with a lack of closure. She looks for ways she'll celebrate retirement and ritualize the transition to a new beginning.

As Linda transitions out of corporate life, she sees plenty of opportunities, from freeing up physical space by getting rid of textbooks, to freeing up time. Instead of filling time with multiple commitments, she is looking for less scheduled time and more spaciousness.

Looking to the future, Linda sees a good variety of flexible activities around her passions. She's glad to have things to keep her active, sharp, and motivated.

Lessons learned: It's important to think about your retirement purpose and have a little bit of a plan and see it unfold. Consider what your spouse is doing in retirement and how you can support each other's retirement in positive ways.

Make Retirement Your Own

Jan's à la carte retirement menu includes time to contemplate, friendship, reunions, travel, stepping back, and being open to opportunities.

Jan, 63, had a career as an actor, performing on stage in New York and Chicago. She also worked in a social services organization. Although she is beginning her third year in retirement, she keeps the door open for performing in the future.

Jan says that her view of retirement continues to shift. She has travelled and planned vacations that include reunions with friends. She is prioritizing friendships that need to be tended.

The luxury of not needing to structure all her days gives her the chance to take her time and figure out how to craft her life. She appreciates slowing down and considering things without jumping right into something just because it is something to do. Before saying yes, she asks, "Is this something I want to spend time doing?"

Jan spends time in reflection. She likens this to cleaning a slate. She visited regrets and has put them to rest. This brought clarity, relief, and peace. Jan has stepped away, at least temporarily, from some work-related commitments and groups. She's open to what opportunities might present themselves as a result.

"I don't think much about age," she said. "It's taken me a few years into this new life to start to feel happy about retirement. I feel more solid on the retirement journey after taking time."

She does not buy into the stereotypical definition of retirement and sees it more as a transitional time of life. She appreciates what's she's learned so far. Some would call this wisdom.

What does Jan see going forward? More leisure, travel, seeing the world, and performing. She is open to new learning and new relationships. She'd like to simplify and downsize, but not quite yet.

She wants to do more things that are outside of her comfort zone. These activities would create a kind of energy, stimulation, challenge, and satisfaction.

Lessons learned: Take your time to think about it and make better choices for yourself. It's important in this unnavigated territory to keep going and make it your own.

Summary

Each of these women created her own à la carte retirement from selections that are unique, enjoyable, and meaningful. As we might anticipate the sweetness of dessert after a good meal, these women are looking forward to the future with anticipation.

They plan to continue being active and engaged. They plan to pursue what holds passion and purpose. They plan to serve others. They are living what Mary Catherine Bateson calls the age of active wisdom.[2]

This is a time of life to pursue new sources of meaning and purpose and find new expressions in our own lives and in the world.

To feed your future and create your own à la carte retirement, here are a few questions to entertain:

- What values and interests will you continue?
- What passion and purpose will you pursue?
- What relationships will you nourish?
- What adventures will you seek?

About The Author

Virginia Macali, JD, MS, is a retirement transition coach. She founded High Point Transitions to support people in making life transitions that are meaningful and satisfying. Virginia offers Exploring Your Next Chapter to help people create their unique menu for what's next in their lives and retirement. She helps people determine retirement readiness, explore options, and create a plan. She publishes *Book Notes for Your Next Chapter* newsletters. Macali is certified as a retirement options coach and integral coach. She is a licensed attorney who has a master's degree in counseling. She enjoys being her own best client and own best coach at this time of life. Contact her at www.VirginiaMacali.com.

Notes

[1] Chris Farrell, *Unretirement: How Baby Boomers are Changing the Way We Think About Work, Community, and the Good Life* (New York: Bloomsbury Press, 2014).

[2] Mary Catherine Bateson, *Composing a Further Life: The Age of Active Wisdom* (New York: Alfred A. Knopf, 2010).

Deciding What To Do With All The Stuff
By Susan Ackley

In the book *The Retirement Challenge,* I wrote about deciding where to live in retirement. I knew when I finished that chapter that deciding the location and type of property in which to live in retirement was the first step in the process and there was more to consider.

So, once the 'where' decision is made, the next step is a two-pronged attack – searching for a new home in your choice location within your parameters and budget, and deciding what will become of your current residence and all the stuff.

Most of us come to the house-hunting process with great expectations. Buying or renting can be a very emotional experience. When you think about what type of home you want to live in, it is difficult not to suspend reality to imagine your "dream house" or "dream location."

When doing house tours, envisioning the great life you're going to live – seeing your family and friends happily sharing and enjoying the space with you – you can picture sitting on the deck admiring the sunset and cocktails; cooking a delicious gourmet meal in the fully equipped kitchen; the perfectly decorated spacious rooms; walking on the beach; playing golf or tennis nearby; and how that remodel project you might tackle will be easy enough to finish in a weekend. It's a wonderful life in your new home.

The dream of that fabulous life can quickly turn into disappointment and fear – especially when you realize all the stuff you have isn't going to fit.

But, if you have determined your goal is to move, it's probably time to start preparing to leave your current residence. Keep a mindset that you are moving toward something new and exciting, rather than away from something comfortable and familiar, is a positive way to view the process and move towards making your ideal retirement life a reality.

No matter how differently you envision your future or where you decide to retire, you will be the same person after retirement that you were before. The transition doesn't dramatically change who you are, how you look at the world, or how you make decisions. So, how you deal with your stuff won't change either, unless you make the change and feel the relief.

Some General Stuff About Stuff

The average American in an average American home has about 300,000 items![1] American garages are so full of stuff that, often, there isn't room to park a car. Also, when Americans move to a new home, on average, 10-15 boxes remain unpacked for five years or more.

According to Spare Foot's self-storage industry statistics, the United States had 50,000 storage facilities, with 2.3 billion square feet of rentable space, with 90% occupancy

One in every 11 Americans is paying an average of $91.14 per month to rent space, making self-storage a $38 billion industry. Industry growth has risen 7.7% every year since 2012 and investment in storage facility development continues to grow – primarily because the wave of downsizing Baby Boomers needs extra places to put their lifetime of accumulated stuff.

Naturally, situations arise when a storage unit is a necessity. When my husband and I sold our house and our new home was undergoing a remodel, we had to put our stuff in storage while we lived in a Residence Inn. It was a good option for that. But to store the stuff you don't have room for in your home or garage is not ideal.

QuickenLoans.com recommends anyone that has rented a storage unit should get out now. The money site cautions readers that they are fooling themselves that the things they own may one day be valuable.

Additionally, the extra storage allows buying more stuff, which creates a cycle of needing more storage space, which is essentially spending money on stuff not needed, won't use, and can get stolen or ruined in storage. Plus, the fees can be financially draining. Also, missing just one month of fees could put the unit and the stuff at risk of being repossessed and auctioned off, sometimes without you being aware.

Abandoned storage unit auctions to recoup fees and expenses by self-storage facilities is big business these days. Thousands of storage units go up for auction every month.

I found an online site, StorageTreasures.com, that has listings of storage units for sale. I searched within 50 miles of my Illinois zip code and found 346 abandoned storage units being auctioned over the next 12 days. Scrolling through the hundreds of photos of open storage units made me feel that I was looking at a preventable tragedy. Just watch one episode of *Storage Wars* for confirmation of that.

How To Deal With The Stuff – Some Ideas

I have already talked about self-storage units and how they can be a good option for short-term storage with fees paid on time every month.

Another idea is businesses that conduct estate or moving sales. The company comes into your home and prices all your stuff, displays it, advertises it, and has salespeople work the sale for 30-35% of the proceeds. Feasibly, you could pack the stuff you want in a pod and leave the rest for a sale. Check out estatesales.net and enter your zip code to see sales and sellers in your area.

Ask your extended family if they want stuff. Be specific. Have a party and offer stuff to people. Give it away to someone who needs it or wants it. You could make someone very happy. Craigslist also has a free listing area. Consider freecycle.org, too.

I didn't mention a garage sale or house sale that you do yourself. I left that out because they are too much work for too little reward. I decided a few years ago they weren't worth the trouble. But if you know prices and have the time, go for it.

I also didn't mention getting a trash bin. Unless your stuff is damaged, wet, moldy, dirty, stinky, or contaminated, I think donating your stuff to a local charity if it is sellable and clean is a better idea. Goodwill is ubiquitous. Their website has a list of the stuff they accept for donations. Just use your best judgement.

Another good option for dealing with stuff is using a professional organizer to give you the guidelines to make tough decisions about the stuff. The professional organizing industry developed in the mid 1980's and has grown exponentially since then.

The goal of organizing is to help move you from chaos to order, in both your environment and life, by wrangling your stuff (and time) so you can live a more functional, productive, efficient, and happier life.

There are quite a few television productions on the topic of organizing stuff, including *Clean Sweep*, *Hoarders*, *Mission Organization*, and *Tidying Up with Marie Kondo*. Increased media attention is often an indication that the topic is of interest or concern to people dealing with their stuff.

And don't forget Margareta Magnusson's book, *The Gentle Art of Swedish Death Cleaning.* A practical book on minimalism, it is based on the concept that happiness doesn't come from stuff, but relationships and experiences. Death is a difficult subject for some to discuss, so this idea may not appeal to everyone.

What I like best about the concept of Swedish Death Cleaning is that it can be a kindness to those surviving, so they don't have to deal with their loved one's stuff. But it's also a benefit to the people who clean, as they can enjoy the memories of the stuff before they get rid of it.

My Dutch husband tells a story about his mother and a saying she had when people talked about stuff they were leaving to family when they died. I shared it with my own mother and I'll share with you, because it is profound. She would say *"Het is beter om met een warme hand te geven dan met een koude hand,"* which means, "It is better to give with a warm hand than a cold hand."

So Where Does All The Stuff Come From?

It can't be a surprise that we live in a consumer-driven economy. We consume twice the material goods as we did 60 years ago. Companies spend millions of dollars to discover how to motivate consumers to buy their products. Cheap consumer goods helped China become the powerhouse economy it is today.

We buy more stuff than we need because we want it. We can feel compelled to "keep up with the Joneses," want to look cool, or have the latest technology and gadgets. We also buy stuff to fill any available space, then we go out and rent a storage unit for it!

But, when the novelty of a purchase wears off or a newer version is released, we rush out to buy the next best, greatest thing we were influenced to buy. It's a vicious cycle with the mountain of stuff we have growing and growing almost without awareness.

Stuff And The Next Generation

Children leave their childhood stuff at home when they go off to college. Even as adults, they may ask to leave a few boxes at home. But often, all their stuff is abandoned.

If your children don't want their own stuff, they want your old stuff even less. Most likely household chattel like furniture, china, crystal, silver, and all that type of stuff will end up either in long-term storage, in an estate sale, an online sale site, dropped at the local charity shop, or in a trash bin.

Your adult children's household choices lean toward Ikea or Pottery Barn and are trendcentric. They aren't trying to hurt your feelings intentionally.

Sentiment isn't an old cedar chest, a set of china, porcelain tchotchkes, an antique breakfront, or the like. Heirlooms, inheritances, and antiques doesn't have value to the next generation, who see it as unwanted old stuff.

My Personal Experience With Stuff

My childhood home was three stories with a full basement. My parents were travelers and collectors, and did a fine job filling every nook and cranny with stuff. Fortunately, my mother was organized, so my family home was filled with organized clutter.

When my parents both retired in their mid-70s, their health required a move to a home without stairs. My husband and I offered to help get their house ready for sale, but neither of us realized what a monumental job it would be.

It took us over a year of evenings and weekends to get it listed. We encountered a huge quantity of stuff. The worst for me was the 255 boxes of books from my father's library, which ended up in storage.

That year profoundly transformed my thinking and perspective on stuff. Seeing all that great stuff ignored and relegated to a corner, closet, cabinet, or box was disheartening and confusing. Was anyone happier because all that stuff was saved and stored?

I am far from a fastidious, organized, everything in-its-place person, but I know that I want to live with quality, not quantity.

Now, most of what I buy is useful and consumable. I recycle and I try not to bring something in without something going out. I prefer experiences as gifts. I keep a box ready for donations. I sell stuff regularly on Ebay or Craigslist. I read newspapers and magazines online. Books are my Achilles heel of stuff, but I read library e-books on my Kindle.

An overflowing box of books I can't bear to part with has been stored under the Christmas decorations for two years. I have an overabundant stock of office supplies, and there are too many straightened stacks of clutter on my desk and credenza – enough paper to drown in!

Working With A Professional Organizer

A few years ago, as my husband and I prepared to downsize to a substantially smaller home. I quickly realized I couldn't tackle the job of sorting, evaluating, and purging half our stuff by myself, so I found an amazing professional organizer, Linette George of Spark Productivity. I couldn't have done the work without her help and guidance. She kept me focused and on task.

Let me share a few of Linette's profound organization questions that are readily on her tongue when working to cut clutter:

- Do you use it?
- Do you need it, or do you want it?
- Do you need more than one?
- "Susan, do you need 30 pairs of scissors?"

- How is that different from that other one?
- If you want to keep it, does it make you happy?
- Do you have a place and space for it?"
- Would you want to donate that?

Feng Shui And Clutter

Feng shui is the 3,000-year-old Chinese system of spatial placement and energy (*chi*) flow within a space. If you have ever felt positive and happy in a space, you have experienced spatial positive chi.

I bring feng shui to you here because I find many overlaps between organizing, staging, and feng shui.

Very simply, feng shui posits that clutter has toxic effects on energy and health. Clearing clutter can promote wellness, positive energy, and happiness. Out of sight doesn't mean out of mind because there is no hiding from low or bad energy.

Here are 10 excellent feng shui tips for clearing clutter:

1. Start small, in one room, and time yourself for 15 or 30 minutes maximum.
2. To declutter a room, start with the worst room first. Use the bin method labeling as "toss," "recycle," "keep," or "evaluate." Touch each item, hold it, and ask yourself when the last time you used it and if you love it. When time is up, empty the bins to their respective homes. Put

the "evaluate" bin in the garage, but if you don't touch it within 6 months, donate the stuff.

3. If you can do only one thing, focus on trash. Walk through rooms with a bag and collect trash.
4. Give away old or damaged clothing or stuff. If an item is broken and can be fixed, fix it or toss it.
5. Sort through any papers on your desk or kitchen countertops. Shred, toss, recycle, or file papers.
6. Let in light and air.
7. The kitchen represents health in feng shui. Clean your kitchen well, starting with the refrigerator.
8. For every item you bring into your home, one item should go out. Learn how to say no if someone wants to give you something you don't want.
9. Evaluate if what you are keeping is only for sentimental reasons, not because you love the item. Is the essence of the person who gave it to you coming through the item?
10. If you have a storage unit and haven't visited it or taken an item out for 6 months, it is time to evaluate, with open eyes, what you are paying to keep, and if what you keep in storage has as much value as the hard work you do to make the money to pay for storage.

There are professional organizers who use feng shui techniques and there are also feng shui practitioners who also clear clutter.

Matt And Janny 2.0

In *The Retirement Challenge*, I introduced you to Matt and Janny and their journey deciding the best place for them to live in retirement. I wanted to tell you more about how they tackled the next steps.

To refresh your memory, Matt and Janny both retired in their mid-50s. I met them when they were struggling with the decision of where to live in retirement and couldn't agree.

Matt and Janny's large home was filled with a lifetime of stuff. Janny had a consultation with the stager a neighbor had referred, and already had a starting point to consign some furniture.

Matt and Janny also decided to use the same real estate broker as their neighbor because of the level of service he gave. The broker was a senior real estate specialist (SRES), which meant he was trained how best to meet the real estate needs of home sellers and buyers age 50 and over. He was able to give the couple a referral to the professional organizer they used.

Once they sold their home, the organizer assisted in packing their old house and unpacking at the condominium. The stager also provided a "staged to live" consultation, which gave their new home the put-together style the couple loved. They both agreed their new home was modern, but comfortable and light – just as they felt.

Conclusion

Matt and Janny used the services of professionals to support them through the challenging and emotional process of downsizing. A coach, a stager, a real estate broker, a mover, and an organizer, all helped the couple meet their goals, and allowed them to keep their stress levels low.

The couple agreed the decision to use professionals also helped them let go of the past and embrace the future with courage.

If you are about to go through a similar downsize like Matt and Janny, but have too much stuff, feel stuck, can't get motivated, or can't make decisions about what to do with all the stuff, help yourself and find a professional organizer for a consultation.

It will still take work, but the organizer acts as your partner and guide, and will provide accountability. It can be a worthwhile investment. If you do, I hope you find someone as great as Linette George. Find more information at www.napo.net/page/howtohire.

If you want to sell your house, consider working with a stager before you list your house. It's work, but staging can and will help your home sell faster, and often for more money.

A stager adds or subtracts stuff from the home's decor to neutralize and enhance the space to appeal to buyers. Going through the process can also help kick start letting of the past. To learn more, visit www.realestatestagingassociation.com.

An SRES is a fantastic resource for anyone 50 or older looking to buy or sell a home. They have the resources to give the best options to help make the life-changing decisions that arise when downsizing and selling your home. Visit sres.realtor/work-sres-designee/find-member for more information.

Asking for help is a strength. Yes, it is true, asking for help is a strength. With too much stuff, or a large home to sell, dated or not, the professionals can be a necessary support for Baby Boomers to get through the stressful, emotional life event of downsizing. Making life easier for yourself is a great way to start being kind to yourself in retirement. You deserve it.

About The Author

Susan Ackley is a certified retirement coach, retirement activist, and charter member of the Retirement Coaches Association. She coaches amazing clients toward finding direction and fulfillment within their retirement journey. Ackley is co-author of *The Retirement Challenge*, published in 2018. She worked in health care financial management and administration for 15 years but returned to graduate school to pursue a new career path in mental health counseling and coaching. Ackley has counseled and coached clients over the past 20 years. She hopes her story inspires clients that reinventing oneself is possible – whether at mid-life or retirement. She lives with her husband, who also reinvented himself at retirement, and their trained therapy dog, a Wheaten Terrier, in the western suburbs of Chicago. In her spare time, Ackley enjoys traveling, visiting hospitals with her dog, reading mysteries, and volunteering. She is developing a group retirement program focused on the nonfinancial aspects of retirement, to allow retiring workers to get their best start in retirement. Visit www.compasspointllc.org for more information.

Notes

[1] Mary McVean, "For Many People, Gathering Possessions Is Just the Stuff of Life," *Los Angeles Times*, March 21, 2014, https://www.latimes.com/health/la-xpm-2014-mar-21-la-he-keeping-stuff-20140322-story.html.

From Apprehension To Achievement: How One Woman Found Meaning In Her Retirement
By Joanne Waldman

After reading an article about retirement coaching, Cathy realized that was just what she needed to support her upcoming journey into the unknown world of retirement. An attorney and corporate executive, Cathy, at 70 years old, retired after several attempts. She had not been looking forward to her retirement as her husband, also an attorney, died 12 years prior, and they had always planned to retire together.

Struggling to find her meaning and purpose, Cathy also felt challenged making the decision as to where to live and felt pressured by her adult children to relocate out of her home and comfort zone to live in another state.

Through diligent and hard work, Cathy, with the assistance of her retirement coach, moved forward designing the life she dreamed of creating even without her husband to share in the outcome.

Beginning The Process

To get the process started, Cathy completed a list of the goals she wanted to reach. These included cleaning up the years of clutter she had been putting off, including cleaning out her husband's desk. Up to this point, Cathy had been too distracted with work and memories to tackle what felt like an unachievable situation. She wanted to focus on her health and get a handle on the extra pounds she was holding on to. Another goal, and perhaps the most pressing for Cathy, was making the decision when to move, as well as where that might be, since her children lived in different states and both wanted her to move to those areas.

Cathy felt her one child was putting more pressure on her to make a quick decision and that child was not understanding of her desires and needs. She wanted to learn how to discuss this situation with her daughter in an assertive fashion and feel that her voice was heard. Cathy stated that she never had taken the time to self-reflect and saw this work with her coach as an opportunity to do so, even though it might be difficult.

Finally, Cathy wanted to understand who she was as a retiree which included finding her authentic self and thus moving closer to God. As a result of the coaching, Cathy hoped to complete a one-year and five-year plan.

The next step in the process included taking the Retirement Success Profile,[1] an assessment developed by Dr. Richard Johnson. The results indicated that Cathy was still taking most of her identity from her work as she had not yet shifted from doing to being. She was concerned about her health, especially the extra weight she wanted to eliminate.

Dealing with change was not a strength for her nor was her ability to live in the present rather than focusing on the past. Since she felt she was going through this alone, Cathy could not see as bright a future for tomorrow and felt her struggles expanding in her life right now.

In addition, the assessment showed that Cathy had some excellent strengths particularly in the area of finances, family, and life meaning. Cathy stated the assessment noted that she was more confident in those areas than she thought she was around her retirement.

Finding Her Voice

Initially, Cathy repeatedly told her coach that she could not make decisions regarding her retirement. Cathy felt lost without her husband and wished she could have his input to make those decisions. Her coach gently questioned that statement, asking Cathy if that was really her truth.

The coach pointed out, as an attorney and an executive, she had made many important decisions over the years. The coach acknowledged her strength and ability to make those decisions and invited Cathy to tap into her creativity and ask herself how her husband could help her make those decisions.

Cathy loved that idea and often used that when she had to make difficult choices. As the coaching continued, Cathy found it easier and easier to tap into her decision-making abilities.

Another instance where Cathy wanted to find her voice and learn to be assertive was in dealing with her daughter about the move. At first, her daughter responded in an irritated fashion when Cathy did not want to discuss moving out of her home and to another city.

Cathy came up with a few responses regarding the move and learned how to say no in a nonconfrontational way. The coach role-played that with Cathy so she could be comfortable when confronted. There was an instance where Cathy finally said, "No," when her daughter asked her to do something she did not want to do.

The hardest word is to say is "no," people often think the world will end if they say that and are often shocked when the other person typically does not get upset! This was a huge win for Cathy. After a while, her daughter started using the phrase, "when *you* are ready to move."

Shifting Perspectives

On several occasions during the coaching sessions, Cathy's coach heard her use the word, "trying." The coach explained the distinction between commitment versus trying,[2] and helped Cathy understand that trying left her a back door to not confront the issues at hand.

Using this verbiage showed that Cathy was not ready to address her actions and feelings to move forward to reach the goals she professed. First, it was important for Cathy to understand what trying meant and then she was able to substitute commitment words including "decide" or "choose" in exchange. She could feel the powerful difference that made. Another word that Cathy used when talking to her coach was "should."

This word comes from someone or something else such as societal norms rather than the individual. To help Cathy better understand this notion, her coach made a bold request for Cathy to place herself in experiment mode for a week. When one is in experiment mode, they cannot fail, just learn and move forward.

Cathy decided that the perspectives she wanted to explore while in experiment mode were, "I am lucky," and "I am blessed." Not only was this thought provoking, but fun. It provided relief from all the pressure that Cathy and others were placing upon her.

While focusing on perspective, Cathy shared that she had at times felt that she had two sides to her personality, one that reflected the Cathy of her childhood and the other a more mature Cathy. She thought more about this while doing some life review exercises and wanted to learn how to integrate the best of both scenarios so that she could enjoy the years to come in a healthier and happier fashion.

During the coaching process, Cathy completed many exercises to help her work through her retirement and come to a better understanding of her needs, and values. One such exercise asked her to look at what she was gaining by leaving her job.[3] Typically, individuals believe that they will lose things like their identity or status. This was a whole new way to process leaving her executive position.

Cathy answered that she would gain freedom to schedule her time as she wished along with the ability to travel as frequently as she wanted. Other gains included volunteering more at the nonprofit organizations she loved, as well as focusing on her health, family, and friends. Finally, this provided more time for that self-reflection Cathy had put off for so long.

Another powerful exercise consisted of reviewing statements about what Cathy was tolerating in her life right now.[4] From those statements, Cathy wrote that she was tolerating the clutter in her house, not updating her technical skills, occasionally beating herself up for not applying things that she knew to her life, looking like she had it together when she perhaps did not, and not deciding the ultimate place to live.

This exercise sparked the notion that she did have some great things she felt good about – including her loving family and friends – as she attended to the softer side of life, her upcoming travel plans, managing her financial situation, the involvement in the volunteer work, and the respect of her colleagues.

When Cathy looked at how she had spent her time before retirement, she realized 80% of her time focused on her career.[5] Now, she wanted to shift that to spending 20% of her time volunteering for the boards and 35% of the time she wanted to spend on herself. This would allow her to focus on her spiritual side and discover her authentic self.

As she reviewed her life accomplishments, themes emerged that would now carry over to help her through her retirement. These included her strong work ethic and desire to improve herself, having gone to law school in her 30s with two small children.

She also came to realize that the love and support her parents provided had always been a constant underlying strength. These realizations felt like the wind to her sails that would help her as she floated through her retirement journey.

Tackling The Clutter

Cathy scheduled several weeks to address the clutter in her home spaces that she had been tolerating for so many years. To do this, she requested the aid of her siblings who came into town at different times and helped her take on the basement, boxes of papers, and various items that were no longer wanted or needed.

This plan succeeded in making the house more livable and felt spiritually uplifting as well. As the clutter left the premises, the more space it allowed

Cathy to evolve and grow, lifting her spirits. However, she still had to clean out and sort through her husband's desk. Her coach suggested a "Tackle It" day where there were three calls scheduled – the first to set up the process and rules early in the morning, the second about three hours later to check the progress and coach through the stoppers and emotions of this looming task, and another call at the end of the day to discuss how Cathy felt and what she learned.

Two days before this meeting, Cathy was called out of town for a family emergency, thus cancelling the desk cleaning. The coach did work with another retiree who wanted to take on her clutter, which is a very common issue for retirees. This client at one time had hired a professional organizer but did not feel that she could afford her now.

So, the coach walked her through a visualization where she imaged putting herself inside the organizers body and looked at the situation through her eyes. This client imaged a plan she thought the organizer would approve and was able to successfully declutter.

When Cathy returned home, she finally set the date to clean out the desk. In advance of the call, Cathy set up boxes for giving away items, for throwing things out and for her children and grandchildren. She felt prepared enough to dig into the desk.

Her coach led Cathy through an exercise where she first looked at the frustrating and sad pieces of the desk cleaning and how those thoughts and feeing manifested physically for her (for example, as a headache or knot in her stomach). Then her coach asked how those thoughts could now become fascinating rather than frustrating.

Cathy decided that meant she wanted to find some fun in the process. When the coach asked her how to make that happen Cathy said that she wanted to play her oldies music and have a dance party while decluttering! Before they hung up, the coach reminded Cathy of her strength and ability to get things accomplished.

When the second call happened two and a half hours later, Cathy had completed the task. She felt the hardest part was just getting started as she had put this off for several years. There were a few bumps along the way, especially when Cathy read some of her husband's writing in book margins – something he did with everything he read.

Tears led to smiles and Cathy learned that she had the fortitude to tackle any other project that she desired to complete for her retirement.

Finding Her Purpose Through Volunteering

As Cathy spent more time in her retirement, she concentrated on volunteering as part of several nonprofit boards that focused on working with girls and toddlers. Cathy used her skills as an executive to mentor and coach the other board members and bring fresh new ideas to the organizations. She even received an award for her work and loved giving the speech at the banquet that recognized her contributions. It felt wonderful to be acknowledged.

Cathy realized she was no longer afraid to get up and give a speech. She discovered she was a storyteller about how to live life and wanted to continue using her knowledge to help others.

Volunteering provided a sense of helping others. Getting involved occupied Cathy's life in a positive way. She did not have the time to feel sorry for herself when she was helping other people and giving her time to what she felt were noble causes that taught values, morals, and life skills to so many children.

Leaving A Legacy As A Grandmother

Not only did Cathy feel that she was leaving a legacy with her volunteer work, but she felt this even stronger in dealing with her five grandchildren, particularly the three boys. Cathy spent time travelling to see them, since they were not in the same geographic location. She scheduled trips and took them to see historic sites or visit with other family members.

Through this process, Cathy realized that she did not want to have all three of them together on these trips at the same time. It was too much for her to handle and she used her new assertiveness skills to say so. When with the boys, Cathy utilized that time to help them and became a moral compass, teaching them life lessons at every opportunity. One of the boys began to call her to discuss situations that would arise, and Cathy felt so grateful he felt safe enough to do that with her.

During one of the coaching sessions, Cathy came up with the idea of having bracelets made that the boys could wear to remind them to be kind and loving to others.

They were excited and grateful to have the ability to look at and touch the bracelets when they wanted to think and do the right thing.

Pulling It All Together

After six months of coaching and feeling more confident and hopeful around her retirement, Cathy found herself 25 pounds thinner than when she started the process! As she took on her challenges and self-discovery, the weight fell off with ease.

Cathy found it easier to make affirming choices around food and was delighted that she could now fit into clothes that she had not worn for several years. She even changed her hairstyle and presented with renewed vitality and attitude.

She no longer used her husband's death as an excuse for not moving forward. Cathy wrote that working with her retirement coach – whom she felt was "non-judgmental, challenging and helpful on both [her] retirement and personal journey" – had been the perfect solution to help her pursue this sometimes nail-biting and confusing process.

According to Cathy, "the most important part of the process was that [her coach] never told [her] what to do but asked powerful questions and offered alternative views to situations."

Although there was still more work to complete, and additional coaching sessions to follow, Cathy felt that she had everything in place to ultimately reach the goal of a satisfying and joyful retirement and was looking forward to completing her five-year plan now that the one-year plan was successfully in place.

And In The End

Having worked as a retirement coach for the last 25 years, I have encountered individuals including my client Cathy, who have struggled with many of the topics included in this chapter. Issues including how will I spend my time, where will I live, and what will my legacy be are just a few of the many that come to the forefront as one creates a new normal in their daily life. To successfully maneuver through retirement it takes patience, courage and a willingness to discover your authentic self. The journey may have stops and starts and can be frustrating at times yet is worth it if you are willing to experience the uncertainty and growing pains that it takes to live fully. It helps as Cathy found, to have support, encouragement and acknowledgement from a coach to make this process easier.

About The Author

Joanne Waldman possesses 30 years' experience in transition management, career development, coaching, and retirement. She has an extensive background as a webinar leader, training coaches with International Coach Academy, Coaching Cognition, and for 14 years as director of training with Retirement Options. She is the owner of New Perspective Coaching where she works with Baby Boomers looking to plan their reinvention into retirement. She is a licensed professional counselor and a nationally certified gerontological counselor. A professional certified coach through the International Coach Federation and board-certified coach, she was selected the Career Practitioner of the Year by the National Career Development Association in 2009. Contact her at 314-469-3288 or joanne@newperspectivecoaching.com.

Notes

[1] Retirement Options, *The Retirement Success Program-The Retirement Success Profile,* https://www.retirementoptions.com/our-assessments/retirement-success-profile/.

[2] Coaching Power Tool from International Coach Academy 2001.

[3] Retirement Options. "The Retirement Success Program-Exercise 1-2: I Don't Know if it is Good or Bad, I Just Know I Have to Retire,"

Retirement Coach Training Manual (2015), www.retirementoptions.com.

[4] Thomas J. Leonard and Byron Laursen, *The Portable Coach: 28 Surefire Strategies for Business and Personal Success* (New York, NY: Scribner, 1998).

[5] Retirement Options. "The Retirement Success Program-Exercise 6-2: Life Energy," Retirement Coach Training Manual (2015), www.retirementoptions.com.

Smart Goals For Retirees And Those Who Want To Unretire
By Joe Grant

"Goals are for adults as rules are for children."

— *Morris Shechtman*

If there ever is a book written about retirement that has a one-word-title, I suggest here and now that it be entitled *Don't*. This is not an indictment of those who are happy in their adult years. It *is* an admonition to those who believe that there will never be any problems or challenges, as we look to our outer relationships, nor any aberrations of inner motivation processes.

Stated simply, while you are in a good place, prepare for the worst and expect the best. Develop resilience in your health and your wealth. Then, as the inevitable occurs, you will be a happier person knowing you are up to the challenge!

There will be different navigation required, and this brief chapter is designed to stimulate your thinking toward structuring a future you prefer. You do have some influence over it, while acknowledging that you do not have complete control over anything except choices you make today.

In a few minutes, we will discuss a process that lots of company project managers have used for years: SMART Goals. Namely there are ways to set goals that increase the chances of favorable outcomes — not guarantee them.

What is guaranteed by this process is learning better how to live, whether the specific goal you originally set is fully met or fully failed. Failure becomes *energizing playful learning* instead of angst producing. Curiosity can be trusted, not squelched.

However, there is a tendency to think about these criteria, developed and honed by many fine managers, as *not* relevant to personal goals and the way to steer towards eventual positive outcomes *on a personal basis*.

As a coach to financial services professionals and small business owners, I saw terrible cases of poor business results but also personal despair. When this was the prevailing attitude, there was no blending of personal and business motivation, poor follow up, and a cynical attitude about the idea that goals can be so very positive, so beneficial to happiness and creative achievement.

So, before we really dig into your *preferred futures*, get your mindset right or just don't bother to read any further. You are wasting your time. Find some other author in this book that seems more relevant, right now. They are all interested in helping you!

If you are still with me and want to go on, but are sort of mildly in the dumps or discouraged about goal setting, here's some pick-me-ups.

Here are some books you can read about this:

- *Mindset*, Carol Dweck

- *One Small Step Can Change Your Life*, Du Maurer
- *The Retirement Challenge*, Retirement Coaches Association
- *Atomic Habits*, James Clear
- *Laws of Lifetime Growth*, Dan Sullivan

And here's a YouTube search that could help: "How to find your life's purpose in 5 minutes or less"

If you feel you are mildly optimistic and don't need them right now, just move on, but make a note to buy them for your library. If you don't have a library that is personal to you, it is like having no friends as you age.

The most powerful influences on you as you attempt to age well are the books you read and the people you meet — sometimes one can be both. But it is hard to set goals unless you are feeding your brain and exercising your brain at the same time. So, now I'm assuming you are ready to create your preferred future, and curious about what it might be!

First, get a piece of paper. I like to buy three-hole punched paper because it discards as easily as paper that is not punched, but if I want to save something it is easy to put it in a binder. It's a small step for the long haul. Now, draw vertical and horizontal lines to divide the page into four quadrants. Label the quadrants as Personal, Business, Activities, and Relationships.

Business is an area you may be leaving, so you could just put "volunteer work" there and it will work fine.

However, more and more retirees are moving from one career to another, doing it several times, and starting over and over again. (See *Shifting Gears*, a great book by Langworthy and Duckworth.) Here is the point: Your personal/business goals are like a teeter totter — sometimes one is more emphasized than the other, and habits are formed accordingly.

Those thought patterns or habits are interrelated in many ways and, like a teeter totter, always moving up or down, seldom balanced perfectly, and always influencing each other. You can't pick up one end of a stick. Nor can you easily have one side of a teeter totter.

Practically speaking, this duality manifests itself in observable performance. People who exercise, for example, generally will do better over time in their work (volunteer work or for profit) than others who let themselves go physically.

Personal disciplines carry into work arenas and vice versa. An exhausted single mother or father cannot bring the full force of their brain to bear on some arena other than home. Work and home are always interrelated.

Next you have Activities and Relationships to consider, so label those quadrants, and we are ready to roll.

The Smart Formula

Specific: The more specific the goal is stated, the easier it is to remember and to have both sides of your brain engaged. If both sides are synched, it seems logical to assume that momentum is easier to get and maintain. Incentives, too, must be personalized.

For example, golf played for $10 per hole is different than purely social golf, and is different than tournament golf. The *size* of the challenge must be considered, and then the risks suited to the individual. A 90-year-old cannot become a race car driver, although my great-great-uncle Pete thought he was at age 92.

We rode with him one day, and it was the worst scare of my life! Yet, in retirement, we want to have enough risk that we are piqued, energized, and curious. All of these thoughts occur as internal dialogue before they become an external commitment. How scary is it?

If you feel some emotion stirring, or maybe some fear, then you are getting specific to *you*. Your vision can be specific in terms of place, emotions, senses, and people. It will be easier to fit into, easier to prepare for. Be specific.

Measurable: Almost anything can be measured, either directly or indirectly in its effects, so the mistake here is to blandly label something that *screams* for a way to ensure progress. Avoiding measuring is a sure way to eventually screw up your outcomes with lousy follow up.

Your habits will not be formed sufficiently to support your goals in the long run. And then achieving isn't fun! Your subconscious needs fun (dopamine) to keep going. So figure out some good ways to measure your fun!

Attainable: Here is the problem: You can't fly to the moon now. Some years from now, it may be possible with the right vehicle and your body being in great physical shape, but that isn't possible *now*. And your prefrontal cortex, along with your subconscious, *knows* that.

So how can you really expect to make the goal happen if you don't believe it will? If you think you can or think you can't you are right. To get the motivation juices flowing, and the right attitude powering you onward, belief becomes critical in your self-talk. Set the table with attainable goals.

Relevant: Here is where you have a chance to "fix" things in advance. Good criteria will support the entire process. Doing a goal is achieving the goal, with failures included. What if you are learning to improve your tennis game when you are really all about shooting your age in golf?

Often people will think that multitasking can work to "get there." Multitasking will get several things done at one half to one third the effectiveness of doing the tasks separately. But you can *leverage*. Do conditioning exercises that complement the other achievement areas you have.

Brooks Koepka, the two-time U.S. Open champion, works out early before his golfing round — not during it. But the two activities complement each other within the daily envelope. Another way to leverage is with other people — an art class can open ways to vary or improve style or find new mediums of expression. Are your goals relevant to each other and complementary to the end game?

Time: Without a proper time frame, you will have trouble visualizing it happening in a practical way! Visualize your future circumstances and achievements, particularly at night, and your subconscious will often "pop" out a part of the vision that could be accomplished within a short time period. Think about the third criteria – attainable.

Believing is important and seeing is believing. These verbal cues to your subconscious can work well, given the right mindset and environment. Whether you think you can or can't becomes your truth or your compass.

For example, could you buy a self-driving car to get you to the grocery because you don't like to drive in inclement weather? Maybe. Teslas have the self-driving option and are available now. You would need the money and the motivation.

But if you want it for tomorrow's sale on fresh cantaloupes, there's no way it will happen – even if you visualize all night long – unless the dealership is next door. But wait, Tesla doesn't have dealerships! Time is important to envisioning the outcomes in a believable way, so get it right. If it is too big too soon, split it up into slices until it fits the vision.

Let's look at the rest of the quadrant zones as we try to put what we've discussed into meaningful goals for adults as they age effectively and joyously. To do it, I like to move clockwise from Personal at the top to Business/Volunteer, then to the bottom where you can put Relationships and Activities.

As I move around the clock, I can sense if this is feeling right, intuitively. Go through it a few times to see what you think and consider the following questions

- Does this feel right to me *now*?
- Who should I be asking about this *now*?
- What roles will I play to be relevant to others?
- How can I contribute (*goals within roles*, perhaps)?

Once you have done this you will have a beginning, not the final answer. You can get your "final" answer when you have been through it several times *if* you are already good at the process. If not, here is what I suggest: First, talk to friends and share it. Help them try to set their own goals.

As you try it, you will get better at your own. Next you could hire a coach — likely a retirement coach, who works with adults past age 50, on what your unique retirement goals could be. Hire a coach jointly with someone else, then have joint coaching sessions.

Third, do online assessments designed for the purpose of creating retirement plans – not financial plans, but *retirement living* plans. Fourth, get more books on retirement and keep reading. Fifth, become a retirement coach and help others with the process on a regular basis at your church, school, or learning center for adults.

The fastest way to get insight, and one of the best ways to start your goal setting process, is to use the third one – online assessments help you define your own attitude patterns very quickly.

For our purposes, there are a number of free assessments and ones that require a fee because the vendor has a licensing agreement. Any one of them will work to start out, but you should not stop using the idea of assessments (inventory of attitude patterns) as one practitioner calls them. Why? Because you can't see yourself without using something to reflect.

A mirror gives you something to start with, but it is external. You need to find stuff inside. There's a bunch of stuff in there that isn't really harmful, but it is kind of heavy. "I can't, because," is an example of self-talk.

As an analogy, a hot air balloon doesn't rise until we throw out the sandbags holding it down. In annual planning sessions, I used to hear the same excuse year after year (along with new fresh ones that appeared quite creative).

Attitude patterns are often improved or overcome if identified (name the demon) in a way that lets us see it for the sandbag it is. Fear is holding it in your balloon basket, but to get rid of it we need to stop valuing it.

So, you may ask: "If my goals are strong enough, won't they carry me through to completion? Won't my will power work?" I hate to tell you this, but your will power will fade. It always does, unless there is a separate goal set to follow through! And you likely will need some help to get SMART Goals turned into a vision.

To a large degree, becoming "younger" requires reinventing yourself *and* your goals. Who is it that is setting them? Who is achieving them or stumbling along? Do you reset goals quarterly, or yearly? Do you measure them? Can you define aging poorly as having no meaningful goals? I believe that is a great definition.

"Know thyself," said Socrates.

Here are some sources for you to find and inventory your attitude patterns:

- DISC (via TTI Distributors, Wiley, or other vendors)

- Strengthsfinder (Gallup)
- Character Strengths (VIA Institute)
- Retirement Success Profile and LifeOptions Profile

For many other free assessments, visit authentichappiness.org at University of Pennsylvania.

So, here is a story about setting SMART Goals that utilizes most of the elements and criteria, above. It is, additionally, about a person who by all accounts could have packed it in, bought the farm, given up, and pulled the plug.

I don't even think for one moment that it is as hard a life as Abraham Lincoln's. Read his failure list anywhere on the internet and be humbled! But it is a short story full of serious ups and downs and successes, and then more potholes in the road.

- A sickly little boy who was overmothered
- Mother was unhappy because of economic depression and perhaps genetic tendencies to emotional depression
- His Depression-era father overworked and was not around much — kind, but distant
- At 12 years old, almost died from eye infection and would have if penicillin hadn't just arrived.
- At 15, parents divorced
- First wife died when she was 22
- Second wife divorced him when he was 28
- Third marriage was the charm

- Started Commissioned sales business with a friend
- Friend left to go to work with someone else
- Older businessman offered partnership, then reneged
- Started business in another state which did well, then nearly went bankrupt at age 53 when parent company failed
- Executive position lost at age 57 when second large company downsized
- Job hunt failed and, in essence, lost $1 million trying to find a new one when the real estate market tanked
- Borrowed $20,000 from a life insurance policy and started a new business with wife and son
- Financed early years with Social Security payments and consulting contracts
- Sold small-business consulting packages
- Trained and coached financial representatives on ethical sales practices
- Currently semi-retired (whatever that means) with homes in two states that are debt free

Whoops, this is me! What a crazy ride! And, while all that junk was going on:

- I graduated from two of the best schools in the United States — Iowa State University of Science and Technology, and The Wharton School, University of Pennsylvania — with no debt
- I became a lieutenant in the U.S. Navy

- I sold financial services for six years and made the Million Dollar Roundtable for three of those
- I lived in Hawaii for 21 years and created a financial services company from scratch with numerous management awards for best performance
- I became an author, consultant, and speaker trainer
- Credit ratings of my wife and myself are both all over 800 with all three rating bureaus
- I raised two beautiful children and jointly created a 49-year marriage. Yes, the third marriage was the charm! What a woman to share the ups and downs and be by my side!

So, where did I learn the most about goal setting? It was in the dark spots at the bottom of the well. You have to find a way up the sides of it to the light by setting goals in a SMART way. A retirement coach can help you – just look in the national directory and find one near you. And call me at (916) 212-0189.

I love to coach for free, for about 30-40 minutes, to see if you can get along without me. I think you can, so let's find out! But first, start your goal-setting process before you call. You may not even need to call after you get going. I hope so. Our website could help also: https://yourvantagepoints.com

Seneca, one of the wisest Roman elites, said, "If you know not what harbor you are making for, no wind is the right wind"

Set the course, then sail it. Don't withdraw from creating your preferred future. You can do it!

About The Author

Joe Grant is a retirement coach, serial entrepreneur, corporate trainer, Rotarian, and golfer. He earned an MBA from the Wharton School at the University of Pennsylvania. He is a former Financial Planner who, having helped people figure out how to save money, realized at some point that the next big task in life was to know what to do with it and help others know their best selves. For more information, visit www.https://yourvantagepoints.com or call (916) 212-0189.

Women Heroes
By Jodi Murray

Women born between 1946 and 1965 are 21st century retirement heroes, daring to navigate their retirement voyage, and challenging the status quo. Baby Boomer women have been lifelong heroes, having the courage to forge a new vision and path in their roles at home, in their careers, and in society at large. For the first time in history, there is a generation of women who have worked for most of their adult lives.

Women entering retirement are:

- Connected through technology and work experiences
- Managed careers of multiple commitments
- Many had careers in fields such as teaching, nursing or social work.
- More women completed post-secondary education
- Many women were the first only in a company, team or position and broke through barriers and stereotypes
- Diverse family structure such as unmarried, single parents, blended families

As a woman born in 1960, I appreciated the advantages and opportunities that became possible for me. I pursued post-secondary education initially certifying as an optometric secretary. I started my family and found myself feeling unsettled, not wanting this to be my long-term work life. I challenged myself and took the risk in returning to school to study Recreation and Leisure studies. When I returned to school, I was in my early 20s and had a son who was 2 years old. Many gave me push-back about "how could I go to school when I had a young son?" My partner rose to the occasion taking on many of the roles I would have done during the week when I was away at school. I continued to pursue my education returning to complete my M.A. and more recently Retirement and Life Coaching certification. Taking the personal risk and challenging previous generation norms provided the ability for me to shape my identity and personal brand throughout my working career.

This social revolution lays the groundwork for transforming how Baby Boomer women approach their retirement voyage and experience. This juncture is an exciting time, providing new insights, and opportunities for women, but at the same time it can be a daunting and confusing time in their lives.

Many conflicting expectations from previous generations can make the transition into retirement scary and unsettling. In many ways Boomer women are pulled to continue traditional roles in their retirement, as modelled by their mothers. For example, feeling obligated to provide full-time childcare for their grandchildren. Charting their own path may seem out of reach.

This chapter explores steps Boomer women can use to direct their own retirement journey, seeing it as an opportunity to tap into their strengths and personal brand.

Statistics on women and retirement have been invisible in previous generations. Baby Boomer women are heroes, having the courage to navigate unchartered waters, and unlocking past views of what women should do when they retire. They have the opportunity to build the foundation for an epic voyage for themselves and future generations.

Although women have increasingly increased their incomes through market share sources, their economic independence is correlated with their career positions.

Women who have held managerial and professional occupations and have pension coverage are more likely to view the timing of their retirement independent of their spouses' timing decision.[1] Women defining their own retirement is a paradigm shift in our understanding of women and retirement. The decision about retirement planning and timing has become a dual decision between partners or a decision that women are making on their own.

Women, today, seek a life that is fully lived and fully realized. This phenomenon can be linked to a number of factors including:

- Increase of women in the labor force
- Increase in financial stability
- Shared decision-making between partners
- Longer life expectancy

- Improved health outcomes
- Transformations in work driven by globalization
- Growth in recreation and leisure knowledge and opportunities

What is next is the opportunity for Boomer women to create a new sense of identity. Building on previous interests and abilities or shaping new identities can be liberating. Retirement provides an opportunity to seek a life that provides a sense of freedom, no longer defined by previous work positions, nor expectations from the generations before us.

Consider the following question: "What lights your fire when you get up in the morning?" Retired Baby Boom women I have coached have said, "having flexibility and more time to spend doing what makes me happy." They also stressed "having the choice to decide what are priorities rather than following a corporate mission statement of company vision," is what lights their fire. In addition, they indicated, "setting small goals that fit me and what I value is what is important."

Taking the time to consider what your goals are that reflect your strengths, interests, and desires with a retirement coach can be invaluable. Post-career/work life can be enhanced through self-discovery and working through strategies with a coach that puts you in the driver seat and helps get you unstuck or anxious about this phase in your life.

When asked what clients have found invaluable or enjoyable about their work with JEM Coaching, one client said, "an opportunity to reflect on my past work experiences and 'take stock' of where I am now and what I would like to do." Another client stressed, "I am feeling more at peace and excited by the possibilities in this phase of life. I was glad to hear that my coach had sensed a different attitude just from how I was talking about things and the way I had completed the strategy exercises. I think just spending some focused time thinking about this phase and then talking about it with a sympathetic listener helped me to accept where I am in life. Also, to do a little research into things like the general aversion to the word 'retirement' helped to normalize my reactions to the word/concept. It also, helped me to disconnect from the more traditional idea of stopping paid employment and to reframe this time of life as simply another phase."

Transitioning into this phase in many ways challenges women to be their own hero, seizing it as a stage in their lives where they can explore, chart their new path and find the hero within themselves.

Being Your Own Personal Hero

In navigating and directing your epic voyage as your own personal hero, think of yourself as the paddler of your own canoe – you cannot change the canoe.

As the paddler, you make choices and take actions to guide the voyage and influence its direction. As you embark on your voyage, you may have to make alterations due to unforeseen circumstances.

What you choose to build into the experience will draw upon your inner strengths, life experiences, and values. You will have many voyages.

Plan your first voyage then your next will build on your experiences, new knowledge, and life circumstances. The decisions you make and the wisdom you have will guide the overall journey and memories.

Retirement coaching has given me insight into what keeps women up at night and stops them from considering what is important to them and what gives them energy. I believe retirement years are to be spent celebrating your unique you, and is a time for self-discovery. It is a time to recreate and seek balance in your life including spiritual, emotional, physical, intellectual stimulation, and social interaction. Women who have struggled with the idea of retirement, and fear losing their identity and independence, have found the Paddler Planner helps them develop a clearer picture of what is important to them.

Paddler Planner

In our life journey, we have hopes and dreams that are satisfied and some which are yet to be realized. This is a time to celebrate you and all that you are. Intercepting the status quo and sifting through the confusion takes insight and courage. One way to think of insight and courage is to imagine a paddle.

The sections of the PADDLE are:

Past is where we gain our insight; our personal brand, strengths, hopes, dreams and values; what we bring with us to take, change or discard on our voyage.

Attitude is the ability to be optimistic and intentional; having a positive outlook; being open to new ideas. Like the paddle at times we may have to dig in and paddle harder to stay on course, have the wisdom to change course or get back on course depending on life circumstances. Having a positive attitude throughout will help maneuver the paddle forward.

Daydream is what drives us and gives us life balance; being mindful and tapping into our inner self and wisdom; giving ourselves license to realize our dreams and give us vitality. It's the way we get a sense of curiosity and fun.

Direct is the way we determine our goals and priorities; make decisions as we aspire to realize our potential; where we derive joy in life happiness; a sense of belonging and connections.

Life Choice is sifting through the traditional vs. non-traditional views of retirement and having the power to choose what energizes us and provides meaning to us.

Experiences are the way we get a sense of curiosity, creativity, and fun.

The more sections of the paddle we consider, the more clarity we have in how we approach our lives and can enjoy this new beginning with independence and confidence.

Paddler Plan In Action

Peggy Anne had a successful career as a professor in a community college. She resisted retiring too soon because she worried about her work identity, being a part of who she was. She sought out retirement coaching to help her to "clear the fog and fear about the uncertainties of post-career life."

She worked with JEM Coaching. With her coach, she used the Paddler Planner as a tool to create a plan, building on her life experience, desires and strengths.

Peggy Anne's Paddler Planner Experience

Past – Peggy Anne reflected on her career and her personal brand and what is important to her. She took great pride in being family oriented, raising three children who now have careers of their own and she has two grandchildren. She learned through coaching that her strengths are love of learning, teamwork, and gratitude. In her career, her passion was to create curiosity with her students to want to learn and use what they learned in their lives. She would like to continue to make a difference in others' lives, but in new experiences. She does not want to teach.

Attitude – Through coaching she explored how she could utilize her strengths and her passion in her retirement, which allowed her as well to have time for family and her grandchildren, having flexibility in her schedule, and to pursue other interests.

Daydream – Peggy Anne took time with her coach to consider other things she would like to pursue, learn, and try. She thought back to things she enjoyed in her youth that she stopped doing as a result of a busy lifestyle. She reminisced about her love for photography.

Direct – Peggy Anne decided to pursue her photography by learning more about filmmaking and storytelling. She enjoyed learning about her students' lives including their past and what they hoped in the future. She thought she could continue this passion by learning about others who are thinking of retiring or have retired and compile their stories in a video. She has begun a part-time hobby/business which gives her a sense of purpose and meaning, as well as independence while staying true to her values.

Life Choice – Peggy Anne took the time through coaching to determine what her options were, what were important to her at this stage of her life and prioritized. By giving herself permission to set goals and pursue them she is living a more satisfied and fulfilled life. She became her own personal hero by having the courage to step outside her comfort zone by starting something new.

Experience – Peggy Anne's choice to learn a new skill and create videos fulfills her love of learning and sense of creativity and fun.

Retirement or post-career/working life can be a time to reinvent yourself, or take time to enjoy the things you didn't have time to do when you were working. It is an opportunity to continue to grow as an individual.

The following self-reflection questions are meant to be a way for you to start your post-career journey in discovering what this amazing time of life can mean for you. You can further your exploration through working in tandem with a retirement coach to help direct your planning process by using the Paddle Planner.

Self-Reflection Questions

- How will your strengths help you create your next steps?
- What dreams have you had that you have not yet realized?
- What has held you back from being kind to yourself?
- What could you currently do for yourself that would make you happy?
- What name would you give the hero inside yourself that gives you the courage to step outside the box and seek your goals?

- How can you challenge yourself to set a date and plan to make your goals happen?

Having the courage to step outside the box and break the mold of traditional ideals and mindset for women and retirement will have those you know still working wishing they were you. You will be their hero.

About The Author

Jodi Murray (M.A., CANCoach, and Retirement Options Coach) is a seasoned coach, leader, and educator. She lives in small town Southern Ontario with her husband. She has a glint in her eye when she shares a story about either of her two adult sons. She has broken the mold of a "traditional" life journey, returning to school as a mature learner, becoming an educator after a successful career as a recreation leader, and more recently starting her coaching business. Inspiring people to find what gives them energy and tapping into their passion is deeply meaningful to her. She believes our life transition experiences are the essence of who we are and make us everyday heroes! For more information, visit www.jemcoaching.ca or https://www.facebook.com/jemcoaching

Notes

[1] Statistics Canada, *Study: Women in Canada: A Gender-based Statistical Report, 7th edition*, 2018

The Risks Of Social Isolation In Retirement
By Mary Morency and Jeannette Lalonde

She had finally achieved her retirement dream: a lakeside property in the country with easy access to skiing in the winter, cycling and water sports in the summer, and privacy with hardly a neighbor in sight.

For the first few months, she thrived, savoring the quiet, natural surroundings. Once the novelty of this idyllic life wore off, a certain malaise started to creep in; she started to feel a bit down and isolated.

As an extrovert, she realized how much she missed the social interactions that city life and work had brought her. How could this have happened to her dream life? How could she have gotten things so wrong? More importantly, what was she going to do to keep her situation from deteriorating and possibly even sliding further into depression?

It turns out that our friend is not alone in her experience of social isolation in retirement.

Research On Social Isolation In Retirement

Let's first clarify what we mean by social isolation. It goes beyond simply being by oneself or having a solitary life. People who suffer from social isolation are often bored to the point of apathy, dissatisfied with their lives and tend to avoid others, feel useless and may have low self-esteem.

In our work helping over 200 clients prepare for a flourishing retirement, one of the most frequently expressed fears about retiring is potential social isolation.

Our clients recognize that a good part of their social interactions have come from the workplace and fear that they will find themselves feeling cut off from others and isolated once they retire.

Among our clients planning their retirement, 40% have not yet begun distancing themselves emotionally from their work; 33% have not figured out how they will replace intrinsic work benefits such as social interaction; 41% voice concerns about attaining an acceptable level of life satisfaction in retirement.

Research confirms the validity of our clients' fear of social isolation as an impediment to a fully flourishing retirement.

The Harvard Study of Adult Development — popularized by Robert Waldinger's TED talk, "What Makes a Good Life?" — attests to the importance of good relationships and a healthy and happy life in later years.

Over the course of 80 years, researchers followed over 700 men annually to assess the quality of their work lives, home lives and health. Their main conclusion was that close, healthy relationships, more than any other factor, keep people happy and healthy throughout their lives. "Social connections are really good for us and loneliness kills," states Waldinger.[1]

Dr. Richard P. Johnson, who described 15 retirement success factors[2] in his book, *The New Retirement*, shares his recent research on low self-esteem in his latest book, *Freedom from Low Self-Esteem.* [3]

We see some interesting connections between the characteristics of people on the low self-esteem spectrum and those who isolate themselves in retirement.

Dr. Johnson describes people with low self-esteem as hiding behind over-activity to avoid looking inward, practicing "hovering" caregiving for similar reasons, feeling lost in an identity crisis, or simply avoiding others. And, he estimates that almost half of the population suffers from some degree of low self-esteem.

In the following section, we draw on our professional experience and client observations to pinpoint the factors that can potentially increase the risk of social isolation in retirees.

Risk Factors For Social Isolation In Retirement

Self-definition: People whose self-identity is strongly tied to their work find it more difficult to redefine themselves in retirement and build new relationships beyond their social network at work.

Because they struggle to let go of the work phase of their lives and start actively engaging in the next stage, they risk getting stuck in an identity crisis that can result in them isolating themselves.

Health Issues: Closely tied to their fear of isolation, many of our clients fear that a declining health will deter from them getting out, finding new activities and remaining active physically and socially. These fears often become a self-fulfilling prophecy that results in isolation.

This potential to isolate oneself also extends to caregivers looking after loved ones with health issues. As they devote more and more of their time to caregiving, they start to withdraw and stop connecting and reaching out to others.

Mindset: We have found that those who view retirement positively, as an opportunity to try new things and continue to learn and grow, are more likely to reach out to others and flourish in retirement. Conversely, those with a more negative mindset, who see retirement as "the end" and feel their best years are behind them are more likely to struggle making new social connections and risk isolating themselves. As they become more self-absorbed and grumpy about life in general, the people in their lives even start to avoid them.

Relationship Issues: As research confirms, strong relationships are the main contributor to happiness and well-being in later stages of life. And the Baby Boomer generation faces different relationship challenges from previous retiree generations.

First, the divorce rate is on the rise for this demographic group, often leaving individuals not only living alone but having to replace long-term social and family networks connected to their former marital status. This can increase the risk of social isolation.

Second, there is a higher proportion of solo-agers — Boomers who have chosen not to marry or to have children. With a more limited family support system, there is a higher potential for isolation.

Last, and worth repeating, many Boomers have devoted a huge portion of their lives and personal identity to their work and have not taken the time to develop a social network beyond their professional one. Sadly, some of them find that building new relationships later in life is far from easy and simply decide to forego the effort.

Leisure Activities: Many people retire having few or no leisure activities. Because they have not taken the time to develop diverse interests and activities, including ones involving interactions with others, they are more fearful or hesitant to join leisure groups – another recipe for social isolation.

Life Meaning: Facing the existential question of what gives one's life meaning requires courage, curiosity, and a willingness to do some introspection. It may seem counterintuitive to say that spending time alone thinking about one's purpose in life will help ward off social isolation, but in our experience, this is exactly what is needed!

Given what we know about the importance of good social connections in our retirement years, we are not surprised when the light bulb comes on after a period of reflection and our clients realize that other people help give their lives meaning in one form or another.

Real Life Solutions To Social Isolation

Recognizing the importance of strong social connections and acknowledging the risk factors that potentially contribute to social isolation, one could conclude that it is hopeless to think that one can attain happiness and well-being in retirement.

We have collected ideas and stories from clients who have found a way to combat social isolation – Real Life Solutions to Social Isolation. So, time to think outside the box, share some ideas about people's best hopes for a retirement "sans isolation."

Real Life Solution No. 1

Explore ways to learn and grow that will allow you to redefine yourself personally, and if you choose, continue to grow professionally. This is an essential part of letting go of our former work lives and transitioning into the "new you."

We like to share our own experience when speaking to clients on this subject. In our former professional lives, we helped organizations manage change and develop leaders.

We wanted to continue nourishing our passion in this area in a different way. So, *voilà* – as retirement coaches, we now help Baby Boomers manage the transition into retirement and develop the attitudes, skills, and behaviors to flourish in this new phase of their lives. To supplement our skills, we obtained coaching certifications, studied applied positive psychology and resilience, and joined several networks to continue our growth and learning.

In addition to the socialization which our coaching practice provides, we have developed close connections with a number of people from different walks of life who help us nourish mind and soul. Whenever either of us feels the slightest hint of isolation creeping in, we reach out to each other as business partners and to a wide network of stimulating people and information.

Real Life Solution No. 2

Take a close look at the quality of the important relationships in your life, find ways to deepen existing ones and seek new ones.

One of our clients, Jacques, realized that he wanted to renew his relationship with his adult son as part of his retirement plan. His son had recently started a new career as a long-haul truck driver and was looking for a partner. After several discussions, the two of them decided that once Jacques retired, he would obtain his trucking license as well, and the two of them would hit the road together. What a great way to expand one's horizons, build a strong connection with family, and avoid isolation in retirement!

Real Life Solution No. 3

Take concrete steps to improve your energy and well-being at the physical, mental, emotional, and/or spiritual levels. Many people arrive at retirement depleted in one or more of these areas and feel quite powerless. This is when the risk of isolation is the highest. We have seen people take charge of their well-being and commit to not only improving, but building strength. And often there is a ripple effect. You take care of one aspect of your well-being and the others start to fall into place.

By his own admission, Gilbert was a workaholic. He had little time for extracurricular activities and had neglected his well-being at several levels. Nearing retirement, he realized that he needed to take some serious action, starting with a much needed knee operation. With a few retirement coaching sessions underway before his operation, he took the time to rest, reflect, and commit to implementing his improvement plan during his convalescence. He immersed himself in a series of books on thriving in retirement and committed to a journey of self-improvement at the physical and spiritual levels. With a new level of physical strength and personal awareness, he engaged in group exercise activities, made new friends, and found time to travel and visit old friends and family with his wife. He has regained the joy of connecting with people as a result of taking care of his physical and spiritual well-being.

Real Life Solution No. 4

Give yourself permission to play. As we said earlier, many people arrive at retirement with few or no leisure activities. Not only have they not balanced work and play in their lives, they actually feel guilty taking time out for leisure. We invite our clients to create a balanced leisure portfolio – physical, social, creative, spectator, intellectual, and even solitary activities. A variety of leisure activities provides stimulation, motivation, and connection with others – all part of a recipe for avoiding isolation.

Huguette had worked in a variety of administrative jobs most of her career, and by all accounts was quite successful. As she neared retirement, she wanted the next phase of her life to reflect who she truly is. Realizing that she had creative interests and talents, she got involved in art and singing lessons. She also joined a local biking club to expand her social network and keep physically active. She now sings in the chorale of the symphony orchestra in her city and paints on a regular basis. And of course, the biking club continues to give her physical and social stimulation. She now lives a flourishing lifestyle in retirement and will add additional leisure activities once her husband retires.

Real Life Solution No. 5

Find ways to contribute – to family, society, a cause about which you are passionate – and ward off the risk of social isolation.

Ronald and his wife were planning to move to another city for their retirement. He realized that he would need to rebuild his social network and that he wanted to find a way to give back to society. With a passion for extreme sports and for connecting with youth, he decided to approach youth centers in his new city and offer his services to train young people in mountain climbing. He found a way to recreate a social network, contribute to his community and find new meaning in life.

Real Life Solution No. 6

And last, but hardly least, plan your retirement. Yes, plan your life in retirement before you retire! This involves taking time to reflect and do some introspection to discover what is important to you and what will give your life meaning at this stage in life. Then, start taking some concrete actions before retiring. We have found that more than any other solution, this one is mandatory.

At the onset of retirement, most people need to take a break, do nothing for a while, and recharge their batteries. Once this honeymoon period has run its course, people often go through a bit of a slump – a normal phase in this all-important life transition. It is when people stay stuck in their slump and don't have a plan for their next steps that the greatest risk of isolation, and even depression, manifests itself.

In each of the previous real-life solutions, the individuals went through a period of reflection to identify what was important to them and what would give their lives meaning.

Jeannette and Mary identified their passion and identified their strengths to reinvent their careers for retirement and contribute to society and their professional community.

Jacques tuned in to his desire for adventure and a deeper connection with his son and took action.

Gilbert listened to his physical wake-up call and went inward before rebuilding his physical and spiritual well-being.

Huguette thought about her true passions in life before giving herself permission to play and expand her social network.

Ronald matched a passion with his desire to contribute to his community and build a new social network.

And let's not forget our friend at the beginning of this chapter who was feeling isolated living in the country. She actually had done some earlier reflection about her personality as an extrovert and her character strengths, especially appreciation of beauty. Loving kitchen gadgets and decoration items, she found a nearby kitchen and gift boutique and offered her services a few days a week. Not only did this solution put her in contact with the public and a team of colleagues, she discovered that she enjoys selling!

They all took the time to reflect and plan, and have built retirement action plans that will certainly serve them well for many years to come. Regardless of the starting point of their reflection, they all seemed to arrive at a common conclusion: Social connection and healthy relationships are key to happiness and well-being in retirement. And if you are thriving you are less likely to experience social isolation.

We will leave you with a simple quote from one of the early researchers and creators of the positive psychology movement, the late Chris Peterson: "Other people matter."[4] We believe that by espousing to this principle as you plan your next phase of life, you will not only minimize the risk of social isolation in retirement, you will flourish!

About The Authors

Mary Morency and Jeannette Lalonde are active retirees who continue to nurture their passion for applying best practices in organizations and helping people develop. After long careers in human resources management and organizational development, they now assist companies and Baby Boomers plan and manage retirement transitions. To facilitate their own transition, they have continued their lifelong learning into retirement with certifications in retirement coaching from Retirement Options and in applied positive psychology and resilience with the Flourishing Center. Based in Montreal, Canada, their services include face-to-face and virtual retirement coaching and workshops, resilience workshops, and knowledge transfer assistance, offered in English and in French. They can be contacted through their website, www.coachingretraite.ca

Notes

[1] Harvard Second Generation Study, https://www.adultdevelopmentstudy.org/.

[2] Johnson, Richard P., *The New Retirement – Discovering Your Dream*, (Chapel Hill, NC: Career Partners International, www.cpiworld.com, 2001).

[3] Johnson Institute for Spiritual Gerontology & Lifelong Adult Faith Formation, https://www.senioradultministry.com

[4] "Other People Matter: Christopher Peterson's Work in Positive Psychology," *PositivePsychology.com*, July 4, 2019, https://positivepsychologyprogram.com/christopher-peterson-other-people-matter/.

Secrets Of A Retirement Coach
By Loretta Saff

Psst! Come closer. Do you like secrets? I'll bet you do. You probably like to have the inside scoop as you plan your career, your vacations, your life, and certainly your retirement.

Congratulations! Since you are doing the research and being smart about planning your future, I've decided to share with you six of my best secrets that will help you have a successful, more fulfilling retirement! Check them out:

Secret 1: Be the Light.

Secret 2: Be the Bouncer at the Door of Your Mind.

Secret 3: Take Inventory in Your Board Room.

Secret 4: Get to Know You.

Secret 5: Never Take Your Eye Off Your Buckets.

Secret 6: Create a Ritual.

Curious? You're probably wondering what they all mean, how I chose them, and why you should pay attention. Let's explore together.

And, if you are the kind of person who thinks secrets are nice but *science* had better back them up, read on. These secrets are backed up by science.

Secret 1: Be The Light

You know those people who just seem to sparkle? I'm talking about the people who, as soon as they arrive on the scene, they simply light up the room. You want to talk with them. You feel better just being around them. You can be one of those people.

I've made "be the light" – or *having a positive mental outlook* – my first secret because it is the foundation for success along the road to retirement.

When you become more optimistic, you'll find motivation and encouragement within yourself and truly enjoy your interaction with others. Being positive in retirement offers a fresh appreciation for what you have, helps you better recognize gateways to new and exciting opportunities, and it may just keep you young.

Samuel Ullman (1840-1924) understood this. Ullman was an American businessman, poet and humanitarian. He is best known for his poem, "Youth," which he wrote after he retired. Here are excerpts:

Youth

Youth is not a time of life; it is a state of mind; it is not a matter of rosy cheeks, red lips and supple knees. It is a matter of the will, a quality of the imagination.

...Whether 60 or 16, there is in every human being's heart the lure of wonder, the unfailing child-like appetite of what's next, and the joy of the game of living.

In the center of your heart and mine there is a wireless station. So long as it receives messages of beauty, hope, cheer, and courage from men and from the Infinite, so long are you young.

When the aerials are down, and your spirit is covered with snows of cynicism and the ice of pessimism, then you are grown old, even at 20, but as long as your aerials are up – to catch the waves of optimism – there is hope you may die young at (100).[1]

The retirement years are different for different people. Some glide right through and happily tell you that these are the best years of their lives.

Others adore the first three months (the honeymoon stage), enjoying their free time and not having a schedule. Then, they start doubting themselves. They question their decision to retire, and they end up in a funk. They become very difficult to be around, and may lose interest in going out.

A new study at the Harvard T.H. Chan School of Public Health[2] demonstrates the importance of a positive mental outlook — the general expectation that good things will happen.

"We should make efforts to boost optimism, which has been shown to be associated with healthier

behaviors and healthier ways of coping with life's challenges." – Dr. Eric Kim

When I work with clients, one of the first things I ask them is, "What do you really want?" They often pause, and after some hesitation they inevitably sigh and say, "I just want to be happy." But why do they say that? What does this mean?

Maybe it's because most of us grew up on fairy tales. Our parents read the books to us that began "Once upon a time, in a kingdom far, far away...." We always looked forward to the ending: "and they lived happily ever after."

Is "happily ever after" only found in fairy tales? How do you get there – especially in retirement?

People just want to be happy, but they don't always like to talk about happiness. So they scoff and say, "Sure, I use a few smiley-face emojis and clap along with Pharrell Williams. But let's face it, 'stuff' happens. Life isn't roses and lollipops."

No, it's not. So what are you to do if you feel that you just aren't a happy-go-lucky person? How are you supposed to "Be the Light" if your first instinct is to react negatively to problems? The good news is that you can change.

Secret 2: Be The Bouncer At The Door Of Your Mind

Knowing that you can change your outlook gives you the power to push negativity aside. And the idea of being a security guard to your thoughts does have scientific backup.

Dr. Sonja Lyubomirsky[3] is a professor of psychology at the University of California, Riverside. In her research on happiness, she shows that we have more control over how we think than was originally believed

To understand this, draw a circle and split it in half. Label one half 50%. According to Dr. Lyubomirsky's research on twins, 50% of your outlook is genetically determined.

Now, divide the other half of the circle between 10% and 40%. Research says that 10% is random, and the remaining 40% is *choice*. In other words, no more saying you've always been a negative person. You have control of at least 40% of your outlook!

Of course, being happy does not mean that you never experience negative emotions. "Stuff" will still happen, but you will find yourself holding fewer grudges and giving people the benefit of the doubt. You will also be a lot more fun to be around.

Since you do have a choice, consider the next secret.

Secret 3: Take Inventory In Your Boardroom

It is important to take a good look at the people in your inner social circle, or what I call, your "boardroom." The people in your inner social circle are those with whom you spend most of your time. These are the people you call your close friends.

Sometimes you may notice that some of your close friends are really negative. Yes, they are good friends but after spending time with them you leave feeling a bit down.

Researcher Marcial Losada has done studies with psychologist Barbara Frederikson[4] on the effect of negativity.

An interesting result they found is it takes approximately three positive comments to undo one negative comment. (Just think about how exhausting that can be.)

Last week, I met a friend for lunch. I noticed two ladies being directed to a nearby table. As they sat down, one looked around with a scowl and said, "Ugh, it is so dark in here. I'm sure I'll have trouble reading the menu. And why did they give us this table? It'll be noisy near the kitchen."

I glanced at her companion. What would she say? Would she try to diffuse the situation with offers of changing tables and maybe turning on a cell phone light to help with the menu? Or maybe she would suggest they go somewhere else. In any case, she will have to work hard. She will have to make three positive comments to change the negative energy in the air!

Purge your social circles, and make sure your boardroom is full of positive people! If you find that with some this is too hard, limit your interactions with them. Having to constantly change the energy in the air is a waste of time.

Once you've chosen to be more optimistic and spend time with more positive people, what does being "happy" actually mean, especially in retirement? Broadly speaking, happiness includes:

- experiencing joy and contentment
- recognizing what makes you focused and energized
- relating to and doing for others, and
- setting goals and working towards them.

Thanks to Dr. Martin Seligman,[5] there is a lot more science to back up our understanding of happiness and how to get there. In 1998, during his inauguration speech to be president of the American Psychological Association, he surprised everyone by declaring that psychologists have to broaden the way they look at people. He said psychologists are mostly out to fix things, to treat the broken and the desperate.

He encouraged his colleagues to broaden their focus and study life's joys. As a result, today's students can get a master's and a doctoral degree in Positive Psychology.

Secret 4: Get To Know You

Ok, so lots of people are talking about and studying happiness, so what should you do to prepare for and enjoy retirement? That's Secret 4 – *"get to know you."*

Just as your car needs periodic maintenance to keep in top running condition, so do you. Oil gets dirty and needs to be changed. Tires wear down and have to be replaced.

You must periodically examine what keeps you in top running condition. Your beliefs and values are not the same as when you began your career. They need to be examined and often replaced at various stages in life.

But there is no automatic "check engine" light that comes on. Since even more 'stuff' happens as we age, this is a very important time to reassess. Be honest with who you are *now*. Here are some questions and ideas to help you self-reflect:

- When you do a Google Search, what do you type in first and most often? (e.g., sales, weather, vacations)
- If you walk into Barnes & Noble, which section do you gravitate towards? (e.g., self-help, business, non-fiction)
- Try stopping a couple of times during your day and ask, "What would make me feel happy?" (e.g., being alone, joining friends, reading a book)

Many people look at retirement as leisure time — a time to "do what I want to do when I want to do it" — with no plan necessary.

Others already have their list ready – including traveling, writing, starting a business, taking classes, etc. You should have a list. Getting to know yourself at this time will help you make good decisions.

I remember a conversation I had with an acquaintance recently at dinner. I'll call him Ron and simply say that he was a rather critical, somewhat negative person.

When I mentioned that I work with people who are either approaching or already in retirement, Ron said, "Really? You help people get ready for retirement? I'm never going to retire. But I know what to tell them about how to get ready – tell them to write a will! That way there won't be any worries when you keel over at the early-bird special at Red Lobster."

Shortly after that, Ron was forced to retire. I had not seen him since our dinner, and after three months he called me and sounded like a different person. "Uh, hi. Uh, I remember we had a conversation about retirement. Actually, I do think I might need to work with you for a few sessions. This retirement stuff is really hard. It's really boring; I'm smarter than most of the people I know, and actually, I'm pretty unhappy." That's a key warning sign – realizing you are unhappy. So, what to do?

Secret 5: Keep Your Eye On Your Buckets

No, this is not referring to the traditional bucket list of things you've always wanted to do. Instead, these buckets reflect the common areas of Life for most people. (This is a variation of *The Wheel of Life*[6] tool, created by Paul J. Meyer.)

As you get older and more 'stuff' happens, it may be harder to be optimistic. Maybe, like Ron in the story above, you know something is off but you can't quite pinpoint the problem. This exercise using buckets can help:

Draw a circle with eight spokes coming from it in all directions — like a sun and its rays. On the end of each spoke, draw what looks like a bucket. Make each bucket half full, and label the buckets with these areas of life:

- Friends
- Health
- Hobbies (passions)
- Financial
- Family
- Spiritual (core beliefs)
- Contribution (do for others)
- Work (something that makes you feel productive)

Next to each bucket jot down what you think you need in that category to feel comfortable and content. Treat this as the level *you* strive for. There is no right answer, only your *honest* response.

For example, regarding family, you may feel you need to speak to your kids every day to feel good. Someone else may say talking with the kids every other Sunday works out fine. Everyone is different.

"Keep your eye on your buckets" reminds you to check your life buckets once a week to see how you are doing. Decide if you focused too much or too little on a particular area, and adjust accordingly — either in your actions or your needs.

Gaining this new self-awareness builds resilience, which is especially useful as you approach retirement. Accepting that plans made can be plans changed increases your clarity, boosts your confidence, and results in a renewed sense of optimism as you continue along the road to happily ever after.

Secret 6: Create A Ritual

To help you focus on making that positive mental outlook part of who you are, the last secret is to "create a ritual." Since it takes repeating a series of actions for 30 days to result in a habit, I decided to offer a campaign called "Make Happy a Habit," on Instagram (@makehappyahabit). There you can find an encouraging image for each of the 30 days, as you follow these simple instructions:

Make Happy A Habit!

1. When you wake up, say out loud three things you are grateful for.

2. Before you go to sleep, write down at least one good thing that has happened within the last 24 hours.
3. Exercise 20 minutes per day. (If you are too busy for 20 minutes, this can be done in two 10-minute intervals.)
4. Meditate at least five minutes each day. (This can be as simple as closing your door and sitting quietly and listening – really listening – to music without words.) There are many free and easy apps to help. I like headspace (www.headspace.com).
5. Each day perform at least one random act of kindness. (Compliment someone or allow a car in front of you in traffic. Make it a personal goal.)

Brene Brown, social science research professor at the University of Houston, says,

"When you own your own story, you get to write the ending."

Work on making yours "happily ever after!"

About The Author

Loretta Saff is a certified professional life coach and retirement coach. She lives in Nashville, Tennessee. You can sign up to receive her blog and order her three *10 Great Tips* Handbooks (Parenting/Grand Parenting/Retirement) via her website at www.coachingwithloretta.com. Her presentations and seminars are witty and informative, and those who have worked with her privately often comment on her positive outlook and attentive listening style. She helps people in transition, with special focus on retirees. Saff believes we all have our own answers inside ourselves. Sometimes we just need a little help finding them.

Notes

[1] Samuel Ullman, "Youth," https://www.uab.edu/ullmanmuseum/. The original poem, written in 1918, ended with the old age of "80." I have taken the liberty to update it to reflect today's old age of "100."

[2] Karen Feldscher, "How Power of Positive Thinking Works," *Harvard Gazette*, March 4, 2019. https://news.harvard.edu/gazette/story/2016/12/opti stic-women-live-longer-are-healthier/.

[3] Sonja Lyubomirsky, "About the Book: The How of Happiness," http://thehowofhappiness.com/about-the-book/.

[4] "Barbara Fredrickson," *Pursuit of Happiness*, https://www.pursuit-of-happiness.org/history-of-happiness/barb-fredrickson/.

[5] "Martin Seligman," *University of Pennsylvania Faculty Profile*, https://www.authentichappiness.sas.upenn.edu/facu lty-profile/profile-dr-martin-seligman.

[6] "Motivating People To Their Full Potential," *Paul J Meyer*, https://pauljmeyer.com/.

About The Retirement Coaches Association

The Retirement Coaches Association is a group of dedicated professionals who are committed to helping people thrive in this next phase of life! Our goal is to not only help you see and experience retirement in a truly different and more meaningful light but also to help you:

- Formulate your vision for your future.
- Unlock and expand your potential.
- Reinforce and maximize your strengths.
- Formulate a plan to keep you relevant, connected, and active.
- Provide encouragement and objective feedback.
- Develop balance in your life now and in the future.
- Support your efforts and provide you with increased confidence.
- Brainstorm strategies to accomplish your goals.
- Uncover and assist in developing your unique abilities.
- Inspire you toward continuous improvement and unparalleled results.

To find a coach near you or to learn more about the organization and our mission to change the focus of retirement planning, please visit http://retirementcoachesassociation.org